Simon Boas

A Beginner's Guide to Dying

Simon Boas was born in 1977 and spent his childhood in London and Winchester. He spent his career working for development charities across the globe as well as the UN. At forty-six, he was diagnosed with advanced throat cancer. In the year following, he wrote pieces about happiness and illness for his local paper, which went viral, encouraging him to expand. *A Beginner's Guide to Dying* is the result.

Praise for Simon Boas's

A Beginner's Guide to Dying

"Boas's cheerful stoicism seems to have touched the nation."
—*The Telegraph*

"Reading *A Beginner's Guide to Dying* you're struck repeatedly by the terrible juxtaposition of the rush of erudition from this fantastically bright mind still thrumming with life and wit, and the silence of the end, which is so near.... There are wonderful vignettes, beautiful meditations on faith and friendship, advice for the dying and those around them." —*The Guardian*

"As Simon Boas treads the pathway we shall all tread he is funny, compassionate and wise. A book not to be missed."
—Sir Terry Waite

"Simon Boas's outlook on life is an inspiration to us all, and his wonderful book is full of both wisdom and humor."
—Julia Samuel, author of *Grief Works*

"I had the privilege to conduct Simon's last broadcast interview—knowing his wise words on the page could live on afterwards. How lucky we all are to have someone as generous as him to share such important perspectives on life while dying." —Emma Barnett, BBC Radio 4 Today

"Funny, moving, brave, sensible—and without self pity. Simon's book celebrates human resilience and reminds us all to enjoy life while we have it." —Jeremy Bowen

A Beginner's Guide to Dying

A Beginner's Guide to Dying

Simon Boas

Vintage Books
A Division of Penguin Random House LLC
New York

FIRST VINTAGE BOOKS EDITION 2025

Copyright © 2024 by Simon Boas

Penguin Random House values and supports copyright. Copyright fuels creativity, encourages diverse voices, promotes free speech, and creates a vibrant culture. Thank you for buying an authorized edition of this book and for complying with copyright laws by not reproducing, scanning, or distributing any part of it in any form without permission. You are supporting writers and allowing Penguin Random House to continue to publish books for every reader. Please note that no part of this book may be used or reproduced in any manner for the purpose of training artificial intelligence technologies or systems.

Published in the United States by Vintage Books, a division of Penguin Random House LLC, 1745 Broadway, New York, New York 10019, and distributed in Canada by Penguin Random House Canada Limited, Toronto. Originally published in Great Britain by Swift Press in 2024.

Vintage and colophon are registered trademarks of Penguin Random House LLC.

Library of Congress Control Number: 2024050860

Vintage Books Trade Paperback ISBN: 979-8-217-00774-5
eBook ISBN: 979-8-217-00775-2

Author photograph © David Ferguson
Book design by Matt Burne

vintagebooks.com

Printed in the United States of America
1st Printing

The authorized representative in the EU for product safety and compliance is Penguin Random House Ireland, Morrison Chambers, 32 Nassau Street, Dublin D02 YH68, Ireland, https://eu-contact.penguin.ie.

This book is dedicated to my beloved wife Aurélie,
to my parents Anthony and Sarah,
and to my sister Julia

Contents

Introduction	1
Jersey Evening Post Articles	7
'Cancer Penguins'	9
'My Cancer Situation Has Developed Not Necessarily to My Advantage'	17
'My Cancer Hasn't Cooperated'	23
Death and Equanimity	29
Introduction	31
1 Perspective	35
2 Meditation	39
3 Gratitude	43
4 God and Religion	51
5 Counselling	61
6 Others' Grief	65
7 Other People	69

8	Psychedelics	75
9	Miracle Cures, Hope and Acceptance	81
10	Thinking about Death	87
11	Optimism	93
12	Regrets and Bucket Lists	99

A Beginner's Guide to Interacting with the Dying	103
Recommended Reading	121
A Short Chronology	123
Random Facts	125
Epilogue: Excerpts from Simon's Eulogy	127
Final Word	137
Thanks and Acknowledgements	139

A Beginner's Guide to Dying

Introduction

The kernel of this little book is three articles which I wrote for my local paper, the *Jersey Evening Post*, between being diagnosed with advanced throat cancer (in the summer of 2023) and dying of it (in the next few weeks).

I was very fortunate that somehow the second article went viral, and was shared with millions of people across the world. It was picked up by the *Spectator*, the *Daily Telegraph* and the *Daily Mail*, and I read it out on BBC Radio 4's *Broadcasting House* programme. I was inundated with beautiful, heartfelt messages; some just wishing me the best, and many others telling me that my words had helped them. Some were in a similar position to me, and found a measure of comfort in a perspective which suggested that it is possible to approach death with equanimity and acceptance. Others were living busy, healthy lives and were grateful for a reminder that

A BEGINNER'S GUIDE TO DYING

life is truly an amazing, improbable gift, and by focusing on that one could worry less about the ultimately inconsequential things which tend to occupy most of our daily bandwidth. Several told me they'd been inspired to patch up or end certain relationships, or that they'd quit their job, or even that they'd decided to sell their house and go on an adventure.

I had hoped that I might have more time to develop my articles into something quite a bit longer, but unfortunately my cancer was more vigorous and motivated than I was. This is partly down to my Olympic-standard ability to procrastinate – in no way dimmed, I discovered, by the deadline being so demonstrably close and final – but mainly due to my preference for spending my last days in the sun, drinking white wine with my amazing wife. However, what I have managed to do is to expand on some of the themes I touched upon in my newspaper articles. In particular, I tried to consider and collate what *are* the things which have given me such a great sense of peace and contentment, and why dying at 46 really isn't so bad.* It's rather short and scrappy – Montaigne it ain't – but I hope it gives a flavour of how I have approached my illness and

---

* I actually managed to reach 47 thanks to the opiates and dry white wine

INTRODUCTION

death, and perhaps provides some explanation of how it *is* possible to 'go gentle into that good night', while still living and loving life to the fullest extent possible.

I've also included something I wrote to help people behave around the dying. The fact is that many people don't know what to do, and sometimes therefore say or do something unhelpful or even insensitive. Worse, though, is that because they may worry about doing the wrong thing, some people don't even make contact at all. I hope the little pointers I've provided can help them.

I have called all of this 'A Beginner's Guide to Dying' because the intention was to show some of the things that, for me at least, made the road a bit smoother, and the destination a little less frightening. However, in some ways it may be a rather stupid title. Of the three main words, the only really accurate one is 'Beginner'. However much we've seen or thought about death, we're all beginners at it when it's our turn. And I'm certainly a novice at this, which makes it a bit presumptuous to call it a 'Guide'. These are a few random dispatches from the front line, from a curiously clear, intense and liminal period of my life.

And, for that reason, it's also only partly about 'Dying'. I hope you'll find that it's mostly about living and life. Because, in an almost paradoxical way, I've found that having a really positive view of existence has helped me to be completely accepting of non-existence. I don't even really think of them as opposites now. And of course, it may well be that 'we' don't cease to exist when our bodies do – I think that's a very real possibility – but none of us will ever know that for sure. The 'certainties' provided by both science and religion all ultimately rest on us believing something unknowable and unprovable. And that's how it should be.

I actually thought about calling this 'Morphine and Muscadet', as the two have been great companions on this final journey, especially since I took the decision to turn down the brutal last line of chemotherapy that was on offer. My theory that someone should run a clinical trial on their combined benefits for the terminally ill has not been enthusiastically received by my doctors, but after I decided I'd had enough of the more orthodox treatments I found that opiates and dry white wine helped keep me going far better than endless rounds of poisoning and burning.

I also liked the idea of trying to show that this book is pretty light-hearted. I love life. The humble-bragging about some of what I've spent it on in the second newspaper article is only a very partial – and fairly heavily censored – list of my passions and idiocies. (I'm still a serving volunteer policeman in Jersey, though my thrilling days of dealing with minor car accidents, loose horses and

INTRODUCTION

dangerous overhanging branches are now behind me.) I love my wife and my family, my friends and my job and my hobbies, and my scruffy French sheepdog. I love adventuring and carousing and laughing at my own jokes; I love melted cheese and crosswords and bonfires and poems and toilet humour and crafty cigarettes; I love the sweet smell of the sycamores in the water meadows in the autumn.

I'm sorry that at 46 I'm leaving all that, and the thousands of other things which bring me joy. But I'm not depressed about it. My overwhelming feeling is of gratitude, of how insanely lucky it was to have lived in the first place. Humans being humans and you being you relies on a series of almost unbelievably improbable coincidences. And I have also been fortunate enough to see – sometimes in the worst of circumstances, like the three years I spent in Gaza – just how loving and selfless and fundamentally good our fellow human beings really are. Everyone is simply doing their best, and everyone is exquisitely precious.

There are many reasons not to fear death, and I hope that these short articles and thoughts may enable you to let it into your life a bit more. I have found that talking about death, preparing for it and accepting it, have helped me enjoy life all the more, to prioritise the important things over the trivial, and to feel a little more compassion for other people, all of whom are also trying to find sense and meaning in this brief, wonderful journey. However, in recent weeks I have also been given enormous practical help in this final transition by a group of amazing people.

The palliative care team at Jersey Hospice have been outstanding in helping me go on for as long as possible without too much pain or physical suffering. They've kept me out of hospital when possible, and enabled me to carry on doing the things I love. The final decline is fast approaching, and I know that when it arrives I shall be surrounded by love and good humour (and my family and my dog). Having spent most of my life working in international development, I know that I am extremely fortunate to have had this opportunity, which is still available only to comparatively few of us. Therefore, a portion of the royalties from this book will go to palliative care charities, and particularly those which seek to advance this standard of care in places which do not currently benefit from it.

I wish you all every joy in your own paths, long or short. All shall be well, and all shall be well, and all manner of thing shall be well.

Simon
Trinity, Jersey
June 2024

Jersey Evening Post Articles

Reprinted with their kind permission

'CANCER PENGUINS'

First published on 11 September 2023

I have recently been informed that, like it or not, I *have* to go to the South Pole. Or at least, that's the best way I can think of describing what's happened to me in the last few weeks. About halfway through this soggy summer, a surprised doctor confirmed that the weird lumps in my neck were metastasised squamous cell carcinoma, and the reason I'd had trouble swallowing for a year was a tumour in my throat. (I *told* you I was ill, as Spike Milligan wrote on his tombstone.)

This all requires six weeks of pretty exacting chemo- and radiotherapy in Southampton, which is due to start in mid-September. And the best analogy I've found to explain it is that someone has told me: 'Right, Simon, you *have* to go to the South Pole.' I have no great desire to go to the South Pole, and it's not something one does lightly. But most people these days go to the South Pole and come back fine, although it's perilous and you probably lose some weight (and maybe even some toes). However, I'll also get to see some interesting things on the way (Cancer Penguins!) and know myself better when I get back.

So, I'm currently preparing for my unplanned expedition. I'm passing on my work as Director of Jersey Overseas Aid to my amazing team there, and my responsibilities as Chair of Jersey Heritage to my fellow trustees. I plan to keep in close contact with both by radio, but need to recognise there will be times when I'm in a crevasse and the signal is weak.

I am going to lose weight on my trek south, so I'm feeding myself up as much as possible. Bruno's Bakery and the Parade Kitchen are playing their delicious part, and yesterday evening I ate over a kilo of cheese fondue, a personal best. Less enjoyably, I ought to start the journey as physically fit as possible, so the other day I did a press-up. I'll probably do another one fairly soon.

When all is said and done, this trip to the South Pole is a solo expedition. However, there are many people helping me. Cancer.Je has offered me equipment (a phone for cheaper roaming) and even cash if I need it. Meanwhile, MacMillan has been stunningly, humblingly amazing. A

JERSEY EVENING POST ARTICLES

sort of Polar Outfitters, if I can flog this metaphor for a couple more paragraphs. They have supplied so much in the way of mental and physical support. They have also given me all the information I've been craving, and had experts in all aspects of this journey tell me exactly what to expect. I cannot sing their praises highly enough.

I have also had so much support from so many people on this wonderful island. Cancer's a funny one, in that it's a scary thing and a lot of people don't know how to react. But I've shed many more tears of happiness recently, at the affection I'm surrounded by, than of self-pity.

Thanks to my day job at Jersey Overseas Aid, I've long known what a compassionate and generous place Jersey is. I'm so grateful to everyone who's got in touch, and have resisted responding to the many offers of practical help with a request that my sheepdog's anal glands need expressing (not true, actually, though you'd do it too, you lovelies!). If it's not too depressing, I shall keep you posted from time to time as I pick my way through the snow and ice.

I fully intend to follow in the footsteps of Amundsen rather than Scott, and a cure is definitely possible. Nevertheless, with the cancer fairly advanced, I have to accept that there is a decent chance I'll be taking the Room Temperature Challenge rather sooner than I would have liked. I don't know the exact figures and don't really want to at the minute. But they're easily two-bullets-in-the-revolver type odds. Perhaps a couple more.

In one sense this is all fantastically unlucky and unfair. I'm 46, unbelievably luckily married, doing a job I love, and suddenly facing the possibility of my own extinction. I won't pretend a note of self-pity hasn't occasionally found its way into the songs I sing myself at 4 a.m. And I must also admit to hearing a few bars of anger at that hour too: at taking more than a year to be diagnosed, at cancelled scans, bureaucratic errors, information droughts, etc.

However, that way madness lies, and during daylight hours, at least, I'm pretty good at tuning those emotions out. I've also managed – not quite sure how – not to blame myself too much. Three decades of smoking and a few periods of fairly Churchillian boozing can't have helped (though of course some get away with it for much longer). And it's possible also that my sporadic inability to calibrate how worried I should be about my health meant doctors were slow to take new aches and pains seriously enough. But just because you're paranoid doesn't mean they're not out to get you (as the T-shirt says), and just because you're a bit of a hypochondriac doesn't mean you don't have squamous cell carcinoma.

So, I've managed to avoid some of the obvious pitfalls – self-pity, anger, blame – but how does it actually feel to get such a clear view of the scythe? Well, this may sound bonkers, but it's not actually that bad. The *one* thing which makes my eyes leak is the thought of its impact on my loved ones, particularly my beloved wife Aurélie and my parents. The word 'widow' now chokes me up, and it's even worse if I use it as a transitive verb. However, I'm not really sad for myself, or even fearful, and in fact I'd say the feculent prognosis has fertilised some green personal growth.

So, with apologies for inflicting them on you, stand by for some clichés. You've probably heard them before, and the oldest and truest part of you knows all this anyway, but our busy lives and brains are good at obscuring these thoughts. Cancer has clarified them for me.

First, I have much developed my ability to prioritise. Important things: Love; Kindness; Meaning. Not important: Money; Status; Validation. It's so easy to forget that the truly rewarding things in life are basically free. Moreover, in Jersey, we are all richer than almost any human being who has ever lived. We have guaranteed access to shelter and food, and to health care and education and justice. We can instantly communicate with anyone, travel anywhere on the planet, and we have the entirety of humanity's knowledge in our pockets. In Jersey we live in one of the most caring, safe and close-knit communities in the world. Yet we are usually on a treadmill to acquire more, and we compare ourselves to the few who we think are better off rather than the billions who are poorer. I do not lie awake now worrying about the mortgage.

Second, I have found it much easier to see the best in people. I usually walk around St Helier beaming like an idiot anyway, as I'm hopeless at recognising faces and prefer to baffle a stranger than snub a friend. But since my diagnosis I feel kinder, and swifter to excuse. Sit in the radiotherapy waiting room with people from every background and you realise that much more unites us than divides us (despite the best efforts of extremists on either end of the spectrum).

Observe the little acts of tenderness, the stoic humour, the courage. Serious illness and its familiar equestrian companion are great levellers, because they remove the masks we all wear and reveal the vulnerable humans underneath. And it's quite easy to extend that outside the oncology department to realise that *everyone* is basically just doing their best. Even the woman who pinched your parking space, and the medic who insisted you only had acid reflux!

And finally, with the future uncertain, one lives more fully in the present. One can still worry about what comes next, of course (and I've just learnt the word 'scanxiety'). But I am also appreciating so many things I might not

JERSEY EVENING POST ARTICLES

otherwise notice or feel grateful for. A happy dog stretching in the grass; a perfect mushroom; a really good Stilton! Little things bring me enormous pleasure at the minute (and God I'm going to miss cheese when the feeding tube goes in). Conversely, not being able to make plans removes any temptation to scheme, covet or fret.

What I really wish is that I'd understood all of this many years earlier. With any luck I'll recover, and have decades benefiting from (and annoying others with) these insights. And it is my sincere hope that some of you lovely people might reach these conclusions too, while there's plenty of sand in your hourglass.

'MY CANCER SITUATION HAS DEVELOPED NOT NECESSARILY TO MY ADVANTAGE'

First published on 11 February 2024

My favourite bit of understatement ever comes not from a Brit or a Spartan but from the Japanese Emperor Hirohito. In August 1945, following Japan's defeats in every recent battle and the obliteration of two cities with nuclear bombs, he broadcast that 'the war situation has developed not necessarily to Japan's advantage'.

Well, I'm sorry to have to announce that my cancer situation has also developed not necessarily to my advantage.

Last September, I described in these pages my diagnosis of throat cancer, and likened my upcoming treatment to a journey to the South Pole. Sadly, although the chemo and radiation did a good job on the tumours in my throat and neck, my lungs are now riddled with the bloody things. The prognosis is not quite 'Don't buy any green bananas', but it's pretty close to 'Don't start any long books'.

So, it seems I'm going to hop the twig, and probably sooner rather than later. But many things give me comfort at the minute. The huge support and compassion which my wife Aurélie and I have received from friends, neighbours and even total strangers. My job, which I'm so lucky to love. (I'm still working every day, but quite often leave at 3 p.m. for a pint with someone. The rules are different in Cancerland!)

And there are three related thoughts I have again and again, which bring me joy, and I am writing this to share them with you.

First of all, I take comfort from the thought that I've had a really good – almost charmed – life. (I'll start this piece with the boasting, in the hope you will have forgiven or forgotten it by the end.) I have dined with lords and billionaires, and broken bread with the poorest people on earth. I have accomplished prodigious feats of drinking. I have allocated and for several years personally delivered at least a hundred million pounds' worth of overseas aid. I have been a Samaritan and a policeman, and got off an attempted-murder charge in Vietnam (trumped up, to extract a bribe) by singing karaoke in a brothel.

I have climbed the Great Pyramid, sailed across the Med and chipped chunks of concrete off Checkpoint Charlie. I have travelled extensively on five continents, sung in choirs on three and crossed borders with diplomatic immunity. I have seen whales and tigers and bears in the wild. I have seen air strikes, rockets and gun battles, the despair of the bereaved and the vacant stares of the ethnically cleansed. I've rolled a car, been shot in the leg and pulled one of my own teeth out. *The Times* has printed seven of my letters,* and I am currently vanity-publishing an exceptionally rude poem about cyclists.

Most of all, I have loved and been loved. I'm cocooned in the stuff; my cup overfloweth.

At 46, I have lived far longer than most of the humans in the 300,000-year history of our species. So have you, probably. And if the book of my life is shorter than many modern people's, it doesn't make it any less of a good read. Length and quality are not correlated in lives any more than they are in novels or films. So carpe that diem and keep it carped. And enjoy the tiny ways you can make other people a little happier. That's actually the secret of being happy oneself.

My second comforting thought is this: nobody knows whether there's a God, or an afterlife, but it seems unlikely

---

* Eleven now!

to me that our existence is merely a brief and random flash of consciousness between two eternities of nothing. A benevolent creator strikes me as no more far-fetched than the latest efforts of physics to make sense of our world: for example, that volume is illusory and the universe is really a hologram, or that there are infinitely many universes all existing in parallel. Our almost-instinct may well be almost true: what will survive of us is love.

And finally, the thought I keep coming back to is how lucky it is to have lived at all. To exist is to have won the lottery. In fact, there are so many bits of extraordinarily unlikely good luck that have occurred just for us to be born that it's like hitting the jackpot every day of the year. Consider some of them:

There is something rather than nothing. The laws of physics, the strengths of forces, the mass of an electron are poised precisely so that stars and planets can form. Inanimate stardust somehow combined to become self-replicating, and then somehow developed further into eukaryotic, complex life. And then complex life didn't just stop at ferns and fishes, but evolved into creatures that were aware of their conditions. Matter became conscious of itself.

Of all the billions of people in the world, your parents met and merged. And of all the sperm and eggs they produced – this is a billion-to-one shot just on its own – the only two that would make *you* fused and multiplied. If the moment you were conceived had been any different at all – a week later; a bottle of Blue Nun soberer – you wouldn't have been born.

To the staggering improbability of you just being here to read this – in physical and biological terms – is added our good fortune in where and when we live. To update Cecil Rhodes, to have been born in Western Europe is itself to have won first prize in the lottery of life. And we live in the longest era of peace in human history, where our chances of dying from disease or violence are lower than ever before. We also live in an age of extraordinary abundance, the poorest of us richer than any medieval king in terms of access to food, energy, care, transport, knowledge, justice.

So, if I whine that my life will have been shorter than many modern people's, I am massively missing the point. I've existed for 46 years. It's as churlish as winning the £92m Euromillions jackpot and then complaining bitterly when you discover that there's another winning ticket and you'll only get half the money.

Life is inordinately precious, unlikely and beautiful. You are exquisite. When you say – as you do, 20 times a day – 'I'm fine', realise that you don't just mean 'I'm adequate'. You are *fine*. Refined. Unique. Finely crafted; fine dining;

fine china! You really are fine in that sense too. We say it all the time, but unknowingly we speak the truth.

We should be dazzled by our good fortune – dancing on the tables every day. And I mean to keep dancing in whatever time I have left here, and (who knows?) perhaps afterwards too.

'MY CANCER HASN'T COOPERATED'
First published on 13 May 2024

In February, I wrote about my terminal prognosis, and how there were several reasons not to be too gloomy about it. Astonishingly, it ended up reaching many more people than usually read the *Jersey Evening Post*. It has brought me huge pleasure to know my words have resonated with so many people in so many countries, and for quite a while I even managed to write back to all those who contacted me directly.

Several suggested that I should write something longer, and that became my intention. I wanted to expand on some of the points I made – about gratitude and perspective, about the unlikeliness and beauty of life, about kindness, and about the inherent fineness of all the creatures (ourselves especially) who ride this merry-go-round together. I wanted to tell a few stories against myself, just so that nobody was in any doubt about the clayiness of my feet. And, most of all, I wanted to try to explain this apparent paradox: that it is possible to leave life with a sense of equanimity not because one is fed up with it, but because one loves it so much.

Unfortunately, it seems I can't do this. I'd hoped that some last-ditch immunotherapy might buy a little extra time, but my cancer hasn't cooperated. Instead of shrivelling like a vampire in sunlight it appears to have acquired some kind of horse, and has been galloping all over my body sowing new tumours. Liver, spine, pelvis, sternum, various soft tissues, more lung; not quite A.A. Gill's 'Full English' but certainly the ingredients of a cheap hotdog. I've been in hospital with various tedious complications, and although I may try one final experimental drug it seems I will be joining the choir invisible even sooner than I'd thought.

So, this is a last missive, in which I want to try to set out some final thoughts. First of all, though, I'd like to thank the many thousands of people who've commented on my articles so kindly or written to me so profoundly. I've been so buoyed by your love and support, and it just confirms my strongly held view that people are fundamentally good. To take the time to reach out with compassion to a complete stranger – opening your heart, suggesting things that might help me physically or spiritually, sharing your own thoughts and experiences – this is a truly selfless act. I'm just sorry to say that from now I probably won't be able to reply, but your words have brought me great joy.

So, instead of a book called 'A Beginner's Guide to Dying' (stupid title, really; 'Cheer Up, You Buggers' might have been better), I'll sign off with a few final thoughts. Apologies that, summarised and stuck together like this, may come across as a bit trite, but they join my February sentiments in representing much of what has helped me to feel so peaceful and contented.

First, please don't fret too much about the state of the world. Nature will recover from the indignities we've chucked at it, and humans have kindness and love at their very core. Even those who do terrible things were themselves once innocent children, and have been hurt by something they didn't choose. Evil is not a noun, it is an adjective. We should revel in the sheer good fortune of our being here at all, in our pied beauty, and in our extraordinary ingenuity. To steal a line from a recent Reith Lecture, we are a species that has created both the Large Hadron Collider and the Eurovision Song Contest! We have so much to appreciate, so many absurdities to laugh about, and so much in common.

Second, every single person has made a huge difference

to the world. You don't have to have been a philanthropist or a politician or a captain of industry. George Eliot captured it beautifully in *Middlemarch*: 'Her full nature ... spent itself in channels which had no great name on the earth. But the effect of her being ... was incalculably diffusive: for the growing good of the world is partly dependent on unhistoric acts; and that things are not so ill with you and me as they might have been, is half owing to the number who lived faithfully a hidden life, and rest in unvisited tombs.'

All our tombs will be unvisited in a few short spins of the rock around the star, but the smile you gave the checkout lady might still be rippling forward. Most films about time travel revolve around people inadvertently altering the present by changing one tiny thing in the past, but project that forward: you might radically change the future by changing one tiny thing in the present.

Whenever I hear something like 'the only high I need I get from exercise', I always think 'you should get out a bit more'. But in truth there is a free high available to all of us, perfectly legal and almost instantaneous. Make smiling eye contact with strangers – particularly if they look miserable or haughty or thuggish. Compliment and thank people. Say kind things about them behind their backs. Play a game the next time someone annoys you in traffic, or says something uncharitable, by imagining the ways in which they've had a terrible day, or the awful news they may just have received. Strike up conversations. I've enjoyed many different highs in my sometimes rackety life, and this is the only one with no downside. Exercise included!

Finally, please try not to fear death so much. We hide and run from it; we follow joyless diets, or subscribe to transactional belief systems, or try to drown it out with pleasures and purchases. We change the subject. But without death we are not human. I used to think that death was the frame of our brief lives, but now I see it as the *canvas* on which each of us is painted. Talk about it. Let it help you put your quotidian worries and squabbles into perspective. And accept it. Meditation and (with a guide) psilocybin can help.

I happen to think now that death is probably not the end of our truest selves, but it doesn't really matter if I'm wrong about that. We have always been parts of a bigger whole – a pulse in the eternal mind, no less – and, consciously or not, as atoms or as angels, we will return to it.

May your own end be decades away, may you people the earth with your courteous offspring, and may you feast and laugh and voyage and sing! I wish you every joy in all of it. And for those that are interested, once you've sorted the immigration formalities with St Peter or Charon, I hope to be waiting with a Scrabble board and a bottle of Muscadet.

A BEGINNER'S GUIDE TO DYING

Oh, and PS: my filthy poem about cyclists is now illustrated and hidden somewhere on Amazon. Please don't be offended if you manage to find it (I used to cycle too!), and please don't read it if you are put off by the most robust of all Anglo-Saxon swear words... xx

Death and Equanimity

INTRODUCTION

I have been so lucky in these last few months, with death now almost part of the family, to have felt such a great sense of calm and equanimity – even of contentedness. I've got some ideas about why this should be the case, but I thought that for my own interest as much as anyone else's benefit I would try to assemble them in one place. And I've been really fortunate to have had a little more time to do so; in May (writing my final *Jersey Evening Post* article from a hospital bed) I didn't think it would be possible, but I rallied a bit and, although I'm going downhill again quite quickly, it's now June.

I do hope that what I've written here can provide a few pointers, but of course everybody is different and will find that things resonate with them differently. Or not at all. My primary fear in doing this is that anyone who is facing a similar prognosis will somehow feel that they are doing things wrong. God, I'm sorry if that's the case: there really is no right way to approach the grave, and the last thing I want to do is to say that there is.

However, I actually think that this little scrapbook may be of more benefit to those whose end is some way off (we hope), and who haven't perhaps given it much thought. There's probably not much here that you can't find in other places (including those glib West Coast self-help books which for some reason constitute the majority of the literature available to airline passengers).* But, for what they're worth, these are the particular fragments I have shored against my own ruin, and I hope some people get something from them.

There are lots of caveats, alongside the fact that these scraps are personal, subjective and far from prescriptive. Firstly, I'm obviously as much of a novice as you are at this dying business, and I may well be talking bollocks. I'm certainly not a psychotherapist, or a palliative care specialist, or a philosopher. I suppose I'm just a reporter from the front line, who has been blessed (as I think many people are when they are close to death) with a curiously

---

* Please, please, may you have bought this book at Heathrow or JFK!

DEATH AND EQUANIMITY

clear view of what has been and what is to come. Death is a wonderful putter-of-things-into-perspective, and I hope that some of that ability to see what's important and what's trivial can be shared with others who do not have weeks to live.

Secondly, this is a really badly researched and referenced book. I've read quite a lot and thought quite a lot and experienced quite a lot, but I haven't had either time or inclination to refer to sources or check too many facts. And whenever I've thought I should probably do so, getting on with living seemed very much more important. So, these are broad brushstrokes, and come with apologies if they are too thin or trite.

Thirdly, although I think I've been unusually blessed in being able to approach the end with a great sense of contentedness (and even joy), I don't want anyone to think I'm living with the cloud cuckoos. I laugh a lot, and have fun with my friends, and even try to enjoy the absurdities and indignities of my various medical escapades (colonoscopies are *fun* with nitrous oxide, and I am proud of my first ever tattoos from the palliative radiotherapy on the bone metastases!). However, I also cry a lot. Sometimes that's through joy, like when I get paintings from my nephews and nieces. But there's also a deep sadness about not growing old with my beloved wife, and the thought of the grief I will be causing her and my family and many others. This is natural, of course, and I don't think any amount of preparation or acceptance can (or should) make it go away.

And lastly, these musings are personal, but they were also partly written from a selfish motive, which is to capture a tiny bit of myself for my loved ones. I imagine even people who don't know me will get a certain sense of my character and outlook from my writing, but I like the fact that this collates a little bit of *me* in one place, in addition to the memories and stories. Furthermore, it's a bit of *me* which – unlike the real one – can be shut at will and left in the downstairs loo.

I haven't intended what follows to be read in any particular order. Some thoughts are long and some are short, and most are probably ultimately quite flimsy. But if they bring any joy or assistance, that makes me very happy.

1 PERSPECTIVE

I think the biggest help of all to me when reflecting on my imminent extinction has been the capacity to put things into perspective. Part of that has been the ability – which I think most people have at the end – to realise what's important in life and what's not. Few people on their deathbeds wish they'd spent more time in the office, or worrying about what other people thought of them, or pursuing hedonistic pleasures at the expense of relationships and friendships. I don't really regret anything from that point of view myself – even the considerable time I devoted to those hedonistic pleasures. But I do wish I'd had this clarity about how to prioritise much earlier in life.

We get one crack at this, and we never know when the scythe may reveal its silver blade. Yet we spend so much of our time bound up in concerns about things which ultimately make little difference. We fret about our jobs and our incomes, even though research shows that, beyond a surprisingly low threshold, an extra dollar buys almost no additional happiness (and can in fact do the opposite – winning the lottery almost always makes people worse off, even in the end financially). We fret about our children, even though research shows that so much of their characters and futures are dependent on their genes and the influence of their peers, not on whether we gave them tennis lessons or pushy tutoring (kids just need love and security, and they'll turn out fine). We fret about what other people think of us, even though actually other people devote much less time to doing so than we imagine.

A *huge* mistake we all make – I think it must be hard-wired into us – is to compare ourselves only upwards. Social media probably makes this worse, as we see snapshots of glittering, curated lives in pictures (or read the comical humble-brags on professional platforms like LinkedIn – '*So* honoured to be part of the award-winning team which increased the sales of fortified breakfast cereals to non-binary customers in Arkansas'). But 'keeping up with the Joneses' has probably been with us since the Joneses had a nicer cave. And all of us do it. I've spent the last few years living in a place where there is enormous wealth, and have

DEATH AND EQUANIMITY

seen millionaires been made miserable by the fact that someone has a better yacht. And I've seen people max out their credit cards so they can have the latest Range Rover sitting on their driveway.

Aside from realising that the most important things really are those that money can't buy – a happy family, love, a sense of meaning, a sense of accomplishment, a sense of engagement in something, however small – there is a very easy trick to avoiding this tendency. Compare yourself only downwards. I've been so lucky to have lived and worked a lot in the poorest and most troubled places of the world – Gaza, Nepal, plenty of Africa, for example – as well as spending time volunteering in night shelters and on a suicide helpline in the UK. It's been relatively easy for me, therefore, every time I catch myself moaning about something, to think of someone in a slum in Sierra Leone or a needle-exchange in Glasgow or a bombed suburb of Kyiv and realise how extraordinarily fortunate I am.

I would say that this is one of the simplest ways to be happy. One of the things I was fortunate enough to do was to run a programme which sent people from Jersey to go and work for a few weeks with a charity in a developing country. The volunteers made a huge difference to the communities they helped, of course, but I'd say the greatest benefit was to them. They returned with new skills and friendships and experiences, but most of all they came back with this new superpower: they could immediately contrast their own daily worries with those of people who didn't know if they'd starve if the rains were late again (and yet who still managed to send their smiling kids off to school every day in a starched white uniform).

If volunteering abroad isn't realistic, and if you haven't already, try to experience poverty and hardship in your own country. There's plenty of it. Perhaps you already experience it. And there are soup kitchens and women's refuges and, yes, suicide helplines, through which you can both make a huge difference and equip yourself with some far more valuable reference points than the people you work with or who live on your street. Failing that, just read about it. I don't advise consuming too much news as it's skewed towards the awful, and can leave one hopelessly (and wrongly) depressed about the state of the world. But try to find real examples of those whose cornflakes life has comprehensively crapped in. And then set them against Alfie getting an F in maths, or some bugger reversing into your car in the supermarket car park.

2 MEDITATION

I only came to meditation quite late, and I'm still quite shit at it. I think for most of my life I didn't really understand what it was, thinking of 'mindfulness' as one of those wellness fads like detoxes and park runs, or that it involved long periods of discomfort and boredom sitting on a cushion. Indeed, I even remember flippantly comparing Buddhism to alcoholism (writing that with both you spend long periods sitting in one place, with little concern for personal possessions, wearing a beatific grin and feeling affection for random strangers). However, recently I've learned that it's actually incredibly simple.

The main point about meditation is to show us what life is really like. We spend so long basically asleep, on cruise control, at the mercy of the internal lunatic who is continually pumping distracting and inconsequential thoughts into our head, re-enacting conversations or worrying about things that probably won't happen. Meditation helps us take a step back from this continuous chatter and realise that we are *not* the sum total of our thoughts. Thoughts and emotions arise, and they fall away. The past exists only in our memory and the future only in our imagination. By recognising that, we can focus on the present, let go of worry (and even pain, though I'm not quite there yet), and understand that so much of our suffering is actually made by ourselves, both through our expectations and our inability to see how beautiful we all are at our core.

Meditation is also quite easy when you have a good guide.* Don't be daunted by the misconception that the true benefits require years of work or silent retreats; all you need is to find a reliable ten minutes which you can set aside most days in which to practise. It starts with learning to focus on something easy like the breath, or perhaps the noises in the street outside (it's a myth you need total peace and quiet). Very quickly you can develop the ability at any time in the day just to pause whatever is stressing you or pissing you off, and to return to a sense of peace and

---

* I found Sam Harris's *Waking Up* app to be the thing that really broke through it all for me.

contentment. And although you may never get to the huge sense of detachment, calm and well-being that advanced meditators can reach (I'm a *long* way off from that), you can enjoy other benefits.

For me, these included a better understanding of how self-constructed and illusory the ego is, and how interconnected all life is. There's also huge value in loving-kindness meditation, where you practise radiating good wishes to those around you, and eventually to all people and beings. Interestingly, Eastern contemplative traditions usually start off with feeling kindness and compassion towards oneself, before working out to loved ones, friends, acquaintances, people who you feel a little animosity towards and then humanity as a whole. Western practices follow a similar pattern but don't always start with the self, because so many of us seem to have problems in truly loving ourselves.

I've come to see that, to be truly compassionate towards others, you really need to feel compassionate towards yourself. There are meditation techniques that can help, including visualising yourself as a little child and trying to put the things you have trouble forgiving yourself for into the perspective that, mostly, even if you were wrong and selfish at the time, you were just doing your best. I also found counselling and psychedelics really helpful here, and write a bit about them below. But it's striking how similar this kind of meditation is to prayer, where one focuses for a while on someone else – or a whole group of people – and wholeheartedly wishes them to be free from suffering.

3 GRATITUDE

It is rightly very popular these days to keep a journal of the things one is grateful for every day, and this has huge power to help us realise how good life really is. But I've also found that contemplating two much bigger truths has helped me really realise how enormously lucky I am right now and how lucky I have always been, notwithstanding even the fact that I am dying at 46. These are, first: how fortunate we are to exist at all; and second: how lucky we are to exist when and how we do.

I think, whether you believe in divine creation or solely in physics (though the two are really *not* incompatible), there can be no dispute about how fortuitous it is that we are here today as free, conscious entities, able to think and experience and love. Whether it is because some loving, omnipotent, unoriginated Being consciously decided to make the particular farting, mewling, grasping masterpiece that is *you*, or because a set of cosmic coincidences aligned so perfectly and yet so improbably that Simon Boas resulted, being alive at all is something we don't appreciate nearly enough.

I've always approached this issue much more from the empirical, scientific side, and yet the conclusion is the same. Any physicist can explain the origins of the universe from a description of big bangs and space-time and matter, but will also attest to two things: that none of this would have existed but for some pretty spectacular 'Goldilocks' coincidences (not too hot and not too cold); and that there are myriad things which not only can't be explained now, but which may never be.

The universe is fine-tuned for us to exist. As Stephen Hawking wrote, 'The laws of science, as we know them at present, contain many fundamental numbers, like the size of the electric charge of the electron and the ratio of the masses of the proton and the electron . . . The remarkable fact is that the values of these numbers seem to have been very finely adjusted to make possible the development of life.' There are literally dozens of these, and the so-called 'anthropic principle' (that there would *have* to be, otherwise we wouldn't be here to make that observation) in no way reduces the extraordinary good fortune that the dials

DEATH AND EQUANIMITY

were set like that (at least in the bit of the 'multiverse' that most scientists need if they want to explain it away), and we *are* here to observe them.

Add to that, then, the coincidences that made our own green-and-blue planet possible (literally an aligning of the stars): the 'golden' age of the universe, which exists at the only time that small rocky planets could be formed; our stable orbit at exactly the right distance around the right type of star in the right type of galaxy; plate tectonics, a large moon and an atmosphere. And then, even with the conditions just right, the absolute and still-unexplained miracle that life should form, where (to our knowledge and the puzzlement of Enrico Fermi) it clearly hasn't done nearly as commonly as we might expect. Not just life, but biologically complex, sexually reproducing multicellular organisms, a HUGE leap itself from basic single cells.

Mammals followed, and then monkeys, and then hominins and then us. For me, evolution in no way diminishes us as the most exquisite creatures (perhaps equipped with the greatest computing power) in the universe, and nor does it provide any argument at all against religion. Whether you believe we are its planned, inevitable outcome, or just the accidental result of millions of years of pressures and extinctions and luck, the very existence of humans is something we could be celebrating every day.

And more, our consciousness – the thing that makes us experiencing, subjective, self-aware organisms – is still completely inexplicable. Neuroscientists and philosophers describe it as 'the hard problem'. Some – physicists as well as philosophers – quite seriously speculate that in fact consciousness is an inherent property of all matter, while others (more those marinated in Eastern spiritual traditions, but a fair few Western physicists, not least Max Planck) consider that it's the other way around, and that matter derives from consciousness. Whichever it is, please dwell a little on its wondrousness, and how unbelievably lucky we are to possess it.

Next, then, the thought that puts my own death into perspective is the singular unlikelihood not just of humans existing, but of me being one of them. Richard Dawkins put it brilliantly in *Unweaving the Rainbow*: 'We are going to die, and that makes us the lucky ones. Most people are never going to die because they are never going to be born ... We know this because the set of possible people allowed by our DNA so massively exceeds the set of actual people. In the teeth of these stupefying odds it is you and I, in our ordinariness, that are here. We privileged few, who won the lottery of birth against all odds, how dare we whine at our inevitable return to that prior state from which the vast majority have never stirred?'

DEATH AND EQUANIMITY

The chance of *your* father even meeting *your* mother, and then of the trillion-to-one chance of *that* sperm meeting *that* egg, and surviving to embryo, blastocyst, foetus and then baby (that this is not to be taken for granted is something I am only too familiar with myself, after ten years of fruitless IVF), was astronomically improbable. And then you were born in a place, unlike so many places today (and indeed all countries even a century or two ago), where medicine and care enabled you to live into adulthood. It's worth dwelling on that particular bit of good fortune too.

I am acutely aware that I had one of the best starts in life available even to modern, Western-born humans. I had loving, well-off parents who could nurture and educate me perhaps as well as was possible in the late twentieth century, so I really was unusually privileged. But even acknowledging the enormous hardships which so many others have had to suffer – abuse and discrimination and loss; poverty and violence and uncertainty – I hope it's not too tactless for this white middle-class male to make a few observations about how lucky so many of you reading this have probably been.*

---

* A neurosurgeon called Paul Kalanithi wrote a wonderful book called *When Breath Becomes Air* about his experience of dying of cancer in his late thirties, just before he'd really

It is not the natural state of affairs to live in a society where we can take for granted so many things only dreamt about by previous generations, or those currently growing up in the Central African Republic. In the UK you will not be left to starve or to sleep on the streets with your children. Although it is often poorly provided and very unfairly distributed, you probably have access to pretty decent education and healthcare completely for free. Access to justice too (something often underrated), where you can't be killed or robbed with impunity, and where

had a chance to embark on his medical career. It's a much profounder reflection than this is on life and death, on the future being snatched away, and on what one can both learn and leave behind. It's also beautifully written. However, because he'd had a similarly privileged upbringing to mine, I read one review online which just said: 'Might as well be called "How the Rich Die".' I feel that's a tad mean – I hope Paul has regularly returned to hide the car keys of the reviewer – but I know what's being got at.

The fact is, I *have* been unusually lucky in the circumstances in which I grew up. Private school, Oxford University – and most of all a loving family and one of those marriages which secretly annoy everyone else because we still hide love notes around the house. I also ended up being a very well-paid aid worker (though I've also been broke, and I remember my

DEATH AND EQUANIMITY

you won't be arbitrarily deprived of your liberty or your freedom of speech by a despotic government. In all likelihood, you won't die in childbirth, or have simple waterborne diseases take your toddlers from you. And the sheer number of *choices* you have!

All but the very poorest can choose what to eat tonight from a buffet unimaginable to Louis XIV or a nineteenth-century press baron. Your supermarket contains more products than the larders of the Ritz under Auguste Escoffier. And if you don't fancy that, you can have your food made by a chef and delivered to your door from a choice of dozens of the world's best cuisines. In fact,

excitement when I was offered £800 a month for my first salaried charity job).

All of this, of course, helped me choose the paths I took, which are not in reach of everyone. So, me suggesting that you should try things like travel, psychedelics, volunteering, counselling and bucket lists may stick in the craw if, like so many people, you are struggling to make ends meet. It doesn't feel like I'm being honest if I try to apologise for this, or try to wheedle out of it much more than I did in that last set of brackets, but I *am* sensitive to it. I just hope that the gist of what I'm writing still makes sense, and that you are not too put off by my background. (The morphine, at least, is free, and the Muscadet is £5 a bottle.)

though travel isn't cheap and holidays are out of the reach of many, a lot of people these days can decide to visit almost any country on earth and be there within 24 hours (rather than after ten weeks on a steamer). And you have the entirety of the world's knowledge available to you in the palm of your hand (plus loads of charming videos of kittens). Try to focus on this, rather than the train strike and library closure and the latest uselessness of your stupid local politicians.

We have all won the lottery in life: both to exist at all and to live in the greatest period of abundance in the history of the world. This is why, as I wrote in my second article, that if I should moan that I'm dying at 46 it is as churlish as complaining that I've had to share a £92 million lottery prize with another winning ticket. Our glasses are half full, or perhaps even fuller, and, when we remember this, we should be filled with exuberance and gratitude.

4 GOD AND RELIGION

It's quite a cliché, isn't it, to get terminal cancer and then suddenly to start believing in a creator and an afterlife? It's a bit on a par with that Second World War saying that 'there are no atheists in foxholes'. Some late money for Pascal's Wager (though of all the French theological bet-hedging I prefer Voltaire's, who when asked on his deathbed whether he renounced the Devil responded that now was no time to be making enemies). I could plead that I'd actually reached most of the conclusions below a few years before my throat decided to take revenge for all the crap I'd poured down it, but actually, so what?

I started off life as a Church of England Christian, and when this started seeming incomprehensible my spirituality made a brief last stand and (aged 14) I joined one of

England's sixteen orders of Druidry. I was genuinely interested in nature-based wisdom and the religion of ancestral Britons. But I also wanted to get out of compulsory church attendance at my very traditional school, and took the stance that if the Jews could go to the synagogue and the Muslims to the mosque, then I ought to be allowed to worship in nature on a Sunday morning (preferably with a can of Strongbow). When this appeal was finally denied I instantly 'converted' to Catholicism so that I could go to St Peter's in town, which nobody really checked on, rather than the school chapel. On the Sundays when I thought it expedient not to be caught in bed at 10 a.m. I worshipped in McDonald's.

I went through many years as an atheist, though I think, like all of us, there was always a spiritual organ in there too which could feel wonder and awe and sometimes a deeper sense of connectivity with others and the universe. However, what always kept me adhering to atheism wasn't the transparent hypocrisy (and sometimes harm) of most organised religions (which are just man's inevitably fallible and frequently self-serving ways of interpreting the ineffable), nor was it any great faith that science somehow explained the major mysteries of life and consciousness (it doesn't, and anyway it is not at all incompatible with there being a creator). For me it was the problem of evil.

DEATH AND EQUANIMITY

I simply couldn't get my head around the idea that if there *was* a loving God, how could he possibly allow such terrible things to happen, often to the least deserving people. If there *is* a God, I used to say, then he's a C-word. But, about ten years ago, I found a way of resolving this – and at the same time resolving the actually rather point-missing argument that there's no proof of God – through quite a simple thought experiment which I share below.

Two of the main arguments for atheism (or at least the ones which convinced me) go as follows:

1. There is no proof of God, and in the absence of any evidence it's stupid to believe in him; and
2. Horrible things happen in the world, like children getting parasitical eye-worms and handsome 46-year-olds dying of throat cancer, and that's incompatible with there being a creator who loves us.

These two propositions (there's no God because I can't see him, and there's no God because, erm, wasps) are closely related. If horrible things *didn't* happen, that would essentially be proof that there was a God – or, at least, we'd be living in heaven already. And in any case, if there was any proof of a God, we wouldn't be human (and God wouldn't be God).

Imagine for a minute that God were literally visible to all of us, perhaps as a big white-bearded face on a cloud like a Monty Python cartoon. How would the world be different? Well, first of all, we'd probably do a lot of worshipping. And second, we'd be falling over ourselves to do good deeds. We'd feed the homeless and wash the sick and be jolly sure not to say something bitchy about our boss's increasingly futile efforts to cover up his expanding grey patches. But, although there might be positives – a realistic conviction that death is not the end, and that we'd be reunited with our loved ones in eternal bliss – there would also be very many negatives. Could we ever be sure that someone was doing us a good deed out of the goodness of their heart, or because they wanted the spiritual brownie points? Could *we* ever do something truly good, without knowing it was being performed for the celestial CCTV camera?*

---

* *This*, by the way, is why religion is not only not required for people to act morally, but in some ways is antithetical to it. Are you not cheating and murdering because a set of commandments tells you it's displeasing to (and punishable by) someone else, or because you genuinely understand it's wrong?

DEATH AND EQUANIMITY

A visible (or provable) God would be like living in North Korea. Nobody doubts the existence of the supreme leader, and they fall over themselves doing whatever they think will please him. Now, imagine for a moment that children didn't get cancer. Or – perhaps worse – that they did get cancer but that they'd be cured by enough people praying for them. Goodness me I hate that, grateful as I am for all the wonderful people who've been praying for me. Why should I be cured and an unprayed-for orphan in Malawi die? You can extend it beyond awful illnesses and random, incomprehensible tragedies to the many more minor rug-pullings that all of our lives are subject to. As Michael Bates says in that very un-PC 1970s sitcom *It Ain't Half Hot Mum* (set in the dying days of the Raj), 'Just because you are having beri-beri, and wife is having congress with best friend, it won't stop your house from burning down!'

Even if God were not visibly reclining on a cloud in the sky, if terrible things didn't happen, and humans were not free to inflict terrible cruelties on others, if children were magically saved from car accidents, it would be a short step to deducing that something – God – was preventing it. And then we'd be back to North Korea. The only way we can be truly human, with all of its joys and sorrows, is for bad things to happen for no reason, and for us never to know whether there is a God. Proof of God's existence is therefore not consistent with there *being* any sort of God which humans have ever imagined.

So, this odd theodicy helped demolish some of my main obstacles to belief, or at least stopped me from dismissing the possibility out of hand. And then what convinced me further was actually science. Now, atheists will sneer (as I used to) that God has been in retreat since the rise of the empirical method and our greater ability to explain things which were once mysterious. We no longer need a divine chariot to pull the sun up, and non-believers will say that what remains is the 'God of the gaps', with those gaps being closed daily by advances in physics and biology. But that's not quite true.

I am certainly exposing my ignorance here, and perhaps lack of faith (yup, it *is* faith) that all the remaining questions will one day be answered without any recourse to what we like to call the supernatural. But, for me at least, the more I read about the latest attempts to explain the world and our conscious existence within it, the more I think that none of it seems any more likely than it being the product of a creator.

Newton is long surpassed, and (according to most physicists) so too will be Einstein and space-time. To take a few intriguing modern theories, the universe may actually be

DEATH AND EQUANIMITY

just one of infinite multiverses, each one perhaps diverging from the moment you just tied your shoelace or didn't. We may well be living in a simulation, in which we ourselves are constructs (a proposition developed by Nick Bostrom not merely as philosophical speculation but as an empirical claim with quantifiable probabilities). Or, thanks to an unresolved paradox about black holes and the indestructibility of information, we could actually be living in two dimensions – essentially existing as holograms.

There's been a long debate over whether the weirdness of quantum physics in any way makes the existence of God more likely. A half-educated dying guy, full of morphine and Muscadet, is not going to make a meaningful contribution to that. However, what *is* undeniable is that the very fact that a human* is observing it changes whether a particle behaves as a particle or a wave. Indeed, without interactions it's hard to say that a particle truly exists; it is just a wave function of probabilities. Brilliantly, this also applies outside our concept of 'time', which itself to many physicists is not fundamentally real: we can observe a photon emitted a billion years ago and, by observing it, change not only how it is now but how it has always been.

There is an extraordinary connection between matter

---

* Amazingly, not a camera, unless it is plugged in!

and consciousness.* For me, this all contributes to the feeling that it takes no greater leap (unless one is willingly wishing it away) to think that a loving creator made the universe, and that we are all manifestations of that creative force. Furthermore, *that* makes me think there really is a possibility that something of us lives on beyond the bag of tissues and foibles and hopes we currently inhabit. And our living experience so often points us in that direction too, even if atheists want to close that one down. We *do* experience love, and transcendence, and awe and gratitude and oneness with others and, though none of that proves anything, it certainly makes *me* think that it's not so stupid to believe that there's something beyond ourselves.

Where has that left me? Well, that doesn't really matter in a way. But I suppose I'm at least no longer an atheist, and I'm alive to the possibilities of many other explanations for my existence. Perhaps I'm some kind of 'pan-deist' or 'pantheist', and I'm attracted to the non-dual world views of some types of Buddhism (Dzogchen) and Hinduism (Advaita Vedanta). Either way, I am no longer scared of death as the end of everything (though if you *do* believe

---

* Or at least life, although it's hard to know whether unicellular organisms also influence the observer effect.

that it should also bring no terrors). As I wrote in one of my articles, I used to think that death was the *frame* of everything (rather like that beautiful Anglo-Saxon image of a swallow passing through the brightly lit mead hall, via windows at each end, in brief respite from the cold, stormy night). But I now see death as the canvas on which we are all painted, our non-existence not just intertwined with our lives but a necessary ingredient of them.

5 COUNSELLING

My wife, sister and sister-in-law are all counsellors or psychologists, and not only am I enormously proud of them but, because I took quite a lot of interest in their training and subsequent work, I am also overwhelmingly of the belief that counselling is an incredible thing, and can help literally everybody. Despite this, however, when it came to signing up myself, I was quite resistant. What am I going to *talk* about? I'm not *traumatised*! Yes, I went to an all-boys boarding school in the days when they were still pretty feral, and yes, I've skidded along the borderline of excess in many things, and I've been shot and seen killings and lived in war-torn places and lost windows in Gaza a few times (to both sides equally, as it happens). But I've dealt with it!

Well, coincidentally, I finally decided to find a counsellor about a year before I was diagnosed with cancer, and it was one of the best things I ever did. Amanda was amazing, gently getting me to talk about things I'd never spoken of, and astutely making connections between them. There's no real magic to it, I think; just talking about things can make all the difference. This is also the principle behind Samaritans. Not all callers are actively about to take their own lives, but all are in distress, and after speaking for an hour most are feeling a bit better. They even thank you for your advice, when in fact you haven't given any (and are not allowed to do so). Good counsellors help you see your own options rather than tell you what to do.

My main piece of advice, besides just doing it, is twofold. First, take some time to choose someone you resonate with. There are lots of different styles of counselling (Freudian, person-centred, gestalt, etc) and it's worth doing a little research into the one you think might help you (if you can't pick, humanistic is probably a good starting point). And beware that the word 'counsellor' is not a legally protected term like 'doctor' or 'psychologist' – literally anyone can call themselves one, so it's worth seeing if they've trained properly and are registered with an accredited professional body. But, mainly, try a few, and don't necessarily go with the first one you find.

I looked in a directory of accredited counsellors in

DEATH AND EQUANIMITY

Jersey and shortlisted three I liked the sound of. Some will give you a free first session, but if not it's worth just paying for one. I dodged a bullet that way. I went to see a counsellor who was highly reputed and even had a PhD, and about halfway through the session I mentioned that I was trying a few people to see who I clicked with. 'What?' he said. 'How do you think that makes *me* feel?' I thanked him for giving me such a clear red flag and left feeling it was 70 quid well spent.

The second thing I'd say is 'persevere'. Sign up for at least six sessions and see how you feel after that. One or two won't really get you anywhere at all. And, yes, I know I'm talking from the privileged position of being able to afford it, but (in the great scheme of things) paying a few hundred pounds to potentially transform the way you look at yourself is a better investment than a holiday or a slightly flashier car. And, goodness, when it emerged that I was seriously ill, and then that my visit to Cancerland was a one-way ticket, knowing I had Amanda to talk to was invaluable. Dying brings with it all kinds of emotions – fear, guilt, extreme worry for the people who love you – and putting them into words is one of the best things one can do.

Get over any stiff-upper-lippedness you may still have, or satisfying snobbishness that 'being in therapy' is something for the emotionally incontinent. And don't think that just because you have close friends or a loving partner that *they* can be your counsellor (it's not fair on them, for one thing, although of course such relationships are profoundly important). Find a professional and it can change your life.

6 OTHERS' GRIEF

This is maybe the hardest topic to write about and, as I said above, I think there's probably not much one can really do to prepare for or mitigate it. It has occupied my thoughts a lot over the past months, and still makes me cry when I think about it. I'm happy to discuss almost any aspect of my dying, from the medical to the metaphysical, but the hardest question I get asked is 'How is Aurélie doing?'

The late Queen Elizabeth, one of the wisest and kindest people I can think of, said something very profound on the death of her beloved husband Philip: 'Grief is the price we pay for love.' It is debilitating, hits one unexpectedly at any time and, contrary both to the Victorians and Elisabeth Kübler-Ross, there is no order or time frame for it. However, for most people it *does* pass, or at least it gets put into a manageable place by the green shoots of a new life growing around it. The dead are always there for you, but gradually the 'pain' button is pushed less often when you think about them, and your interests and friendships and sense of meaning grow in the soil which your loved one still partially cultivates.*

There are really good resources available now about grief, and this is not one of them. I have no advice on how to leave your spouse or how to predecease your parents, and, however much I hope that reflecting on my life, and my cheerful leaving of it, may help them in the end, they will be hit by a loneliness that comes from the finality of realising that they will never see me again. And as for leaving children – I would be guilty of a crime if I dared to express anything but a profound sense of compassion and sympathy which I can never fully understand. It was one of our great sadnesses not to be able to have any kids, though one which eventually we came to terms with. It probably makes things easier right now, but it also makes me so sad to think of the gap left by their absence in the future for those who love me.

* I found a couple of simple cartoons which illustrate this well. You might find them if you Google 'grief ball in a box' and 'Tonkin's model of grief' (after bereavement counsellor Lois Tonkin). The idea is that grief itself does not become any smaller, but your life widens around it.

DEATH AND EQUANIMITY

So, what can one do? Trying to ensure that your loved ones have good people they can talk to and who will support them is perhaps something you can help with before you go. Also, to whatever extent it is possible, try to ensure your family knows that they do not have to carry your coffin for too long. They are not a 'widow' or an 'orphan', even though society and well-meaning friends can unhelpfully define them as such. I would additionally say that specialist counselling is really essential, and I have seen how grieving people get a lot out of being around others who are also going through the crippling sense of finality that a death brings.

I am also trying to do some of the deathmin in advance, so that Aurélie doesn't have to.* (I used to think I'd like to die suddenly, perhaps under the wheels of the proverbial bus, but actually – for both practical and spiritual reasons – having a few months to prepare and get things in some sort of order has been a wonderful gift.) It's good to write down all the information about finances, passwords, insurance, etc, and please try not to be among the 50 per cent of

---

* Though I *still* can't change the car or house insurance into Aurélie's name, and two afternoons spent chatting with bots and call centres exhausted even my normally healthy reserves of patience and good humour.

British adults who do not have a will. I've actually found that if one *has* any final wishes there's no need to wait until one is dead to enact them. Give those little treasures away now!

Most of all, though, I think about how I hope people will remember me, which I'd like to be with a big smile on their face. The way I try to conceptualise it for others is by getting them to try to think of me as a book they are glad they've read. All our lives can be thought of as books: for some we are just a paragraph or a footnote, and for others we are a chapter or a volume. But we're not someone's whole book, even our spouse's or our parents' or our children's. We are characters in *their* stories. And they will keep writing beautiful chapters in their own books after we have gone.

Just because someone dies before you, it doesn't change the joy (and pain and exasperation and everything else) that their segment of your book has brought you. Dwell on the quality, not the quantity, and don't fixate for too long on the fact that it ended, just like you don't dwell for too long on the fact you've finished reading or watching something you loved. Just be glad you had them, and that they will be with you forever as a part of your own story.

7 OTHER PEOPLE

I'm going to sound like such a dreadful hippy here, but it needs sharing. It is easy to get high off other people. Not just your friends and loved ones, and not just the people you share activities or interests with. You can walk around a town or a shop or a hospital getting high off perfect strangers. Realising this really changed my life, and it has also been so wonderful in the run-up to my death.

Most of us, most of the time, go through life with the shutters down. I think this is especially true in big cities, although in Cairo or Kigali it is still perfectly permissible to talk to people on public transport and not be thought of as a loon. However, everyone everywhere has a desire to connect with others, and a deep capacity for kindness and love at their core. The idea of us as atomised, self-serving individuals is simply a myth. I've been lucky enough to see it *in extremis*, like in the aftermath of air strikes or car accidents. People mostly drop what they're doing and, often at great personal risk, run in the direction of danger to do what they can to help. I've also been so fortunate to see it in people's reactions to my newspaper articles, where complete strangers took time out of their days to send me comforting and deeply personal words.

I said I wouldn't bother too much about references and books, but one I strongly recommend if you doubt me is Rutger Bregman's *Humankind*. This tells the true story of six Tongan boys marooned on a desert island for months after a fishing trip went wrong, and shows how they co-operated and helped one another throughout until they were rescued. It then shows, through careful research, that humans are hardwired for kindness to others. It debunks various famous experiments (like the Stanford Prison one) and myths (like the 'bystander effect') which purport to show the reverse. For the past 10 years, social science has increasingly shifted its view on this – that *Lord of the Flies* is just a story, and we are all more like those Tongan fishermen.

My own experience has shown this to be true. I've heard hundreds of stories of abuse and cruelty on Samaritans calls, and quite often also talked to the perpetrators (a lot of prisoners phone the helpline too). I've met victims

DEATH AND EQUANIMITY

of torture in Palestine and Ukraine and Sierra Leone, and shared beers with plenty of fighters in the different Palestinian brigades who may have done some unspeakable things (Al-Aqsa Martyrs, Abu Ali Mustafa, even Al-Qassam and Al-Quds – Islamists, who can also be prone to a glass when nobody's looking).* I've spent a lot of time in Rwanda, where both victims and instigators of the 1994 genocide now live side by side thanks to that country's far-sighted *'gacaca'* reconciliation process. And my conclusion is this: nobody is evil.

'Good' people frequently do bad things, and 'bad' people also frequently do good things. But, contrary to what some religions teach (though in fairness to them, perhaps more as allegory than fact these days), I don't think there is any such thing or force as 'evil'. No devil, certainly no hell, and no person – even the usual twentieth-century villains we can all think of – who was wholly or naturally 'bad'. Evil is an adjective, not a noun, and those who choose to do evil things are rightly condemned and punished for them. But if you look deeper, you really do realise that to know all is to forgive all.

---

* I won't name the Hamas minister in Gaza for whom I used the UN's diplomatic privileges to smuggle in bottles of whisky, but it helped ensure their security forces stopped arresting my employees.

Evil acts do not come out of nowhere; they are caused. The usual culprit is some deep hurt or sadness which has afflicted the perpetrator, but ignorance too can take some of the blame. And from realising that, one can build a sense of understanding and compassion literally for everyone. The huge success of restorative justice programmes is a good example. I was blubbing this morning over a newspaper story about a mother who had become friends with the thug who had killed her son with a single drunken punch, and had moved from campaigning to lengthen his prison sentence to giving talks in schools – alongside him – about violence, consequences and forgiveness.

I'm perhaps digressing a little; I'm not suggesting you seek out and engage with every murderer and rapist (although trying to forgive – or at least understand – those who have wronged you will bring you enormous benefits).* However, simply smiling warmly at strangers – perhaps even offering a kind word, or helping a young mum put her

---

* I've recently been practising on the consultant who insisted for a year that I had acid reflux and not cancer, which meant that when it was diagnosed it was already Stage 4, and the employee I fired a few years ago whose reaction to my terminal prognosis was to ask several of my trustees when my job would be advertised!

DEATH AND EQUANIMITY

pushchair in the car – has an enormously powerful effect. First, it puts *them* in a good mood, and they are then more likely to do the same to others. Then, it helps *you*, and you'll find that your spirits are genuinely lifted through the rest of your day. And, finally, it helps everyone, because society is so much better when we trust those around us. And if people are haughty or intimidating or hidden behind the barriers they've erected to protect themselves, so much the better.

Sorry. This makes me sound so saintly, and I'm really not. I can be a colossal arse much of the time, and have certainly hurt several people in ways I deeply regret. But this advice is really true, and I urge you to try it. It is a superpower that everyone can learn.

8 PSYCHEDELICS

There is now a large body of research which shows the enormous benefits of psychedelic drugs like psilocybin (the compound found in magic mushrooms) for a range of conditions. These include untreatable depression, addiction, and end-of-life anxiety caused by a death sentence such as mine. There is also considerable evidence that a high-dose, carefully prepared-for trip can help almost everyone, even those without a particular problem to solve. I was lucky enough to have experienced one about six months before my diagnosis, and then I followed up this year – just before 'advanced' became 'terminal' – with another. I am not going to present all the scientific studies here,* and I'm also

---

* Michael Pollan's superb book *How to Change Your Mind: What the New Science of Psychedelics Teaches Us About Consciousness, Dying, Addiction, Depression, and Transcendence* is a wonderful place to get started.

aware how tedious it is to hear about other people's dreams, but I thought it might be useful to recount a little of my experience and what I took from it, and to provide a little advice for anyone who might consider this path.

The first thing to say is that you should remove any preconceptions you have about psychedelics as illegal and dangerous. They are, of course, but there is a world of difference between doing them in a safe, guided space and farting about with them in a field or at a party. (Or at the mini-golf at Blenheim Palace – I'm very sorry to all concerned.) The incredible power of psychedelics lies not in their ability to warp reality or give you beautiful hallucinations, but in the way that they can temporarily dissolve your ego and quiet, for a while, the Default Mode Network of your brain (that underlying chatter of autobiography and self-criticism that is a bit like living with a lunatic – the bit that causes us distraction and worry and is what meditation also works so powerfully on). Additionally, psychedelics are powerful entheogens, and can give you access to profound spiritual experiences and transcendent, beatific states of mind where you see and feel connected to what is most pure and primal.

Most cultures have a long history of using psychedelics in ritual or healing, even those that don't have methods of inducing similar altered states of consciousness through chanting, dance, breathwork or prayer. Used safely, they are not something to be frightened of, although one needs to approach with caution. The two key things to get right are 'setting' (where and how you do them) and 'set' (your mindset and expectations).

I worked with two experienced guides (a couple, in fact, who were also two of the loveliest people I have ever met). The weekend retreat starts with you getting to know and trust each other through various exercises, and then some meditation whereby you focus on what's to come and try to empty your mind of other distractions. I made an 'altar' with pictures of my family and little treasures which meant something to me (including the UN's *Guide to Safety and Security* for personnel in dangerous postings!). The following day we meditated some more, and then I took a walk in nature to find three items which would represent what I hoped to get out of this experience: something I wanted less of in my life (night-time anxiety about health, ironically, for which I picked a thorn); something I wanted to keep (a sense of playfulness and mischief, represented by a mushroom); and something I wanted more of (compassion for other people, signified by a berry).

The 'ceremony' began on the afternoon of the second day, with three grams of dried magic mushrooms (I would eventually need that topped up to six; I seem to have a ludicrous tolerance for drink and all drugs). The guides sit with you unobtrusively, carefully chosen spiritual music plays on the stereo,* and you put on a blindfold so that your attention focuses inward and not on the surroundings. Now for the really hippy bit, which lasted five hours but which I will summarise ruthlessly.

The first thing I experienced when the 'medicine' kicked in was a huge sense of joy, even bliss. I felt the presence of some sort of guide (which manifested to me as a sort of playful otter), which said 'just enjoy this and stop being so earnest – the lessons can come later'. I laughed and laughed and felt this incredible sense that all was right with the world. I began to look at my own struggles and worries with a huge sense of compassion, and realise that I was just doing my best, and that it was good enough. Soon after, this widened to everyone: they were also just doing their best. It felt like a superpower, and I tried it out on people who had hurt me – and even on Russian military torturers (I had recently returned from Kyiv). I felt an overwhelming sense of empathy for

---

* This was based on the playlist used during King's College London's huge trial of psilocybin for depression. I know the thought of pan pipes and electronically enhanced ethnic chanting can put people off, but I recommend you go with it!

DEATH AND EQUANIMITY

everyone, and this deepened into a great feeling that we are all connected, and that we are all participants in a great cosmic dance, at the very heart of which is benevolence and love.

You may now be spitting out your cornflakes and thinking, 'What a load of tosh.' But all I can say is that it felt completely real, and it stayed with me for months afterwards. I did things more slowly and thoughtfully, I could meditate far more deeply than I'd ever been able to before, and I felt (and still feel) that we are all just leaves on the same tree, which in time flourish and in time fall and decay, but remain part of a permanent, ineffable whole. (A month later I did a three-day Hostile Environments training with the SAS, where they try to put you in all kinds of stressful and frightening situations, and to their annoyance I floated through it so beatifically I was given the nickname 'Gandalf'. Usually preceded by the word 'Fucking'.)

My second experience was different, and I won't bore you with it, but similar enough to reinforce this sense of connectivity and peacefulness, with another glimpse of what might be termed 'the divine'. I also had this incredible realisation (which I used in one of my columns) that not only are all humans exquisite and beautiful, but that we say so every day without realising it. We all say 'I'm fine' when asked how we are, but it's actually so true beyond the quotidian meaning of 'I'm OK (please shut up!)'. You really are *fine*. Expertly crafted, perfectly adapted to your environment, and full of so much potential and compassion and humour and wisdom. Please try to remember this meaning too when you say it!

I highly recommend psychedelics to almost everyone reading this (though it's not advised if you're on certain medications or suffer from certain mental health conditions). You can do them legally in Holland, and I think Spain. Do some research, and go with an organisation where they really properly prepare you (which should include all kinds of questionnaires and interviews beforehand). Also note how much time they spend 'integrating' after the experience: it's important to spend time trying to work out what you've really just been taught, and how that will apply to your life. It's useful I think for everyone to try this at least once in their lives, and the benefit it's given me as I approach death has been enormous. I still have no idea whether there's a creator or an afterlife, but I'm at least open to the possibility, and I can see my existence and non-existence with a great sense of clarity and perspective. It has helped remove any last vestiges of fear about dying.

9 MIRACLE CURES, HOPE AND ACCEPTANCE

These first few paragraphs really *are* directed at those who are also terminally ill, although I hope that others reading them might learn a bit about how to be more tactful around us.

I am now so riddled with cancer that I keep wanting to find someone to play Top Trumps with so I can boast about the size and extent of my tumours. As well as all the soft tissues and organs, and bones from my clavicle to my heel, they bloody stick out of me! I'm not going to pull through this with turmeric, and the gene therapy they're trying might buy a couple of months if I'm one of the very lucky ones it works on. However, almost every day I am sent very well-meant information about both medical advances and fantastic prayer groups or pastors who have cured all sorts of people whom doctors apparently gave up on. There are two boring reasons why this can grate a bit, but also a more important one which I think goes to the heart of how we deal with death.

The first boring reason (and I set this out again below in my short guide to dealing with the dying) is that it really helps me for others to acknowledge and not minimise the fact I'm dying. I like to talk about it, in fact, and I hope that's not just useful to me. However, if others insist I'm curable, or even (unwittingly) that I'm just not trying hard enough to get better, they're not listening. It's easier to sweep these difficult emotions and conversations under the Isfahan rug, but not kind.

The second reason is more theological and more personal. I wrote above that the problem of evil and suffering is ameliorated for me by believing in a creator who does not intervene in concrete ways in the world (except that I can see love and benevolence almost everywhere, especially now the veil is thin!). I don't want to live in a place where God cures one person just because they have faith, or because enough people pray for them, and leaves another to their fate.

Of course, if you are an atheist this is obvious. As Christopher Hitchens wrote when dying, 'To the dumb question "Why me?" the cosmos barely bothers to return the reply, "Why not?"' But I think also if you believe in something divine it is important to get beyond any sense of injustice, of 'Why me?' If you hold out to the end that God somehow did this to you – but could also change his mind! – you will die concentrating on the unfairness and loss, and not on the extraordinary gift we've all been given in the first place.

Most importantly, though, I have found that hope is antithetical to acceptance. I know of several 'bad' deaths, where people have sought cures and miracles almost to the last, even checking themselves out of hospital to do so, and died angry and frustrated as a result. I also see many cancer friends pursuing all those new protocols and experimental drugs and clinical trials for far longer than they probably should. Sometimes that's because of their own fears and sometimes it's because they feel a kind of pressure from loved ones (or worse, doctors) at least to have said they've tried everything. But it leads to emotional (and very often also physical) suffering.

Accepting death is actually something we can all do, and it is life changing. This does not mean welcoming it as the end of life's difficulties, although I understand why some very unfortunate people reach that conclusion and even hasten it as a result. It doesn't mean being indifferent to it, or valuing life less. It just means understanding that it is inevitable, that it's going to happen to all of us (yes, even you, Silicon Valley squillionaires!), and that it is as much a part of life as birth and puberty and unrequited love and joy and all the rest.

I have found Buddhist teaching on this to be very profound. At the heart of this is an understanding that *everything* is impermanent, and by pretending otherwise we cause ourselves suffering. We cling, we crave, we unreasonably expect, we get disappointed. There is great serenity – even enlightenment – to be found in realising that nothing is fixed, that birth and death are all part of a cycle, and even that the thing which we commonly call 'self' is not some changeless observer but something of an illusion when one examines it closely.

Stoicism also has important things to teach us about preparing for and accepting death. Now, I'm really pretty poorly read on this; I am following my lazy decision not to research anything else for these little scraps, and anyway I'm not trying to write an essay. Also, in several important ways I am very far from being a Stoic myself (not least in my lifelong rejection of moderation in all things: my inclination is to cry for madder music and stronger wine until the feast is finished and the lamps expire). However, beyond the tranquillity a good Stoic might feel looking back at a life of virtue, I think there are three useful contributions we can all take from their outlook.

Starting with the one I find the hardest and least useful, Stoics point out that when you're dead you no longer experience anything – no fear or pain or anxiety – so why worry about it? This is logically true, and may help lessen the terror for some, especially if your world is notably demon-haunted, but it is precisely the *absence* of things which most people fear (even if it's not strictly rational to do so). No sight, no sound, no touch or taste or smell, nothing to think with, nothing to love or link with, the anaesthetic from which none come round. Nonetheless, actually *being* dead is nothing to be afraid of.

The second argument is perhaps more useful, and is found across many philosophies and religions. There is nothing we can do about death, so it's pointless to worry about it. A life spent railing against *anything* which is beyond our control will be a frustrating one. Death is the ultimate certainty, and even if we *do* get a bit of extra time from our miserable detoxes and plasma injections and newfound propensity to hold up traffic while dressed in Lycra and riding a children's toy, it probably won't be a *long* time, and one day you'll be where I am now and there will be nothing you can do about it. As the prayer goes, 'grant me the serenity to accept the things I cannot change, the courage to change the things I can, and the wisdom to know the difference.'

The best lesson from the Stoics is *memento mori* – always hold in mind that you will die, perhaps even tomorrow. This doesn't make life pointless; it makes it purposeful. Prioritise, put worries into perspective, don't put things off. Live! It sounds gloomy, but if you can give this thought a tiny bit of water every day it can make your loved ones a little dearer, the colours a bit more vivid, and the stresses a little less important. And when death does suddenly show up on his skeletal motorcycle, for you or someone else, you are a bit more prepared to offer him a cup of tea.

I have found acceptance to be so liberating. As was always going to be the case, and in a way we can do nothing about, we come into being and we dissolve, returning at least to nature and perhaps also into whatever force set all this aflame. Denying it, clinging on, hoping that a new pill or prayer will cure you, works in the opposite direction.

10 THINKING ABOUT DEATH

I suppose I have done quite a lot of thinking about death over the years, and – like the regular *memento mori* of the Stoics – I think it has helped prepare me. It's not always an easy journey, though, and for quite a while it left me with unanswered questions, a degree of fear and a recurring hypochondria which would lead me to insist on imaging and tests every few years while I was actually completely well. (Which is why I can now laugh at the fact that a consultant took a year to diagnose my throat cancer – the only time I actually needed a bloody CT scan!)

Most people don't see death any more, which is a situation unprecedented in the history of our species. Even 150 years ago we would probably have watched our parents die, we might have lost siblings or children to now-preventable diseases, and most people would have died at home rather than in hospital. Most of us also have never had to fight in a war, or known they had 'a rendezvous with death at some disputed barricade'. Many have never even seen a dead body.

I was a bit different, part by accident and part by design. I did my first aid convoy to a war zone in 1993 when I was 16, to a refugee camp near Mostar in Bosnia, where mass graves and bombed-out villages had a profound effect on me. I spent several months in Cambodia as a late teenager, the first time while the Khmer Rouge were still fighting and the second during Hun Sen's brutal little coup, where I was also deeply moved by the Killing Fields and recent genocide that anyone my age or over would have experienced. Living in Vietnam, I gravitated to a small group of American war veterans, who were there trying to lay old ghosts in long-deserted landing zones, and heal their own trauma and guilt.

My career as an aid worker then took me to many places where death – recent or imminently likely – was part of the fabric of life. In poor countries people still bury two of their five children, and I met tired families in remote villages and filthy slums who literally didn't know where their next meal would come from. In Syrian refugee camps, in Ukraine, in Sierra Leone and in Rwanda I made friends

DEATH AND EQUANIMITY

with people who had suffered the most appalling things, sometimes at the hands of their neighbours. In Palestine, which I moved to at the tail end of the second *intifada*, I saw death first-hand on several occasions: the aftermaths of air strikes in Gaza and of appalling bombings in Jerusalem. My own wife was the only survivor of a terrible car accident outside Bethlehem. Someone was once shot repeatedly right next to me, and I held his hand as he died.

Even in Britain I was perhaps exposed to death more than most. I spent four years as a teenager working at a night shelter for the homeless (oh-so-moral, right, though my greatest pleasure was to break out with my motley gang to go begging and street drinking!). The lonely deaths of my heroin-addicted friends – and the even lonelier pauper's funerals I attended – contrasted strongly with the exuberant and gilded youth of my posh fourteenth-century school, where the future was bright and the world was your lobster.

Finally, as a Samaritan these past four years, I have been privileged to be taken into some of the darkest places of the human mind, where suicide for some people appears to be the only way to end their suffering. Several times I spoke to someone just as they were about to end their lives, and on a few occasions I stayed on the line with them as they did so.

So, death has played a supporting role in my own little play, even before I was forced to come to terms with my own. And the two main lessons I drew from what I eventually came to consider a gift were as follows.

First, even more than taxes, I saw how death is inevitable. But I also learned from those for whom death is so much more present than for most of us that this needn't detract from the living of life to the full. Not in a devil-may-care nose-thumbing way, a last whisky before the ship goes down, but in a calmness and realism that I also now see in the oncology transfusion room. Running away from death is not only a waste of energy; it sets life in opposition to it. Which it isn't. Death is a natural part of life, and the more we understand that, the more we can enjoy living.

Second, I learnt of the importance of being with the dead. Almost every other culture I can think of has customs and rituals which involve actively engaging with the departed, from the cremation *ghats* at Pashupatinath to an Irish wake. In Asia and in Africa, graves are cleaned and visited, ancestors are celebrated with wine and gifts, and in Madagascar I've seen parties where the dead are physically exhumed after a few years, wrapped in fresh shrouds and taken to a dance. In Britain and America – if we're lucky – we may have an hour with our loved one before the undertaker is called and we never see them again.

DEATH AND EQUANIMITY

I understand that most people in the West are not going to start digging up Granny for a final game of bingo, and hopefully we won't suddenly be exposed to violence, starvation or plague (although Covid sadly forced a lot of people to confront that last possibility). However, we can let death into our lives a little more, even just by thinking about it rather than hiding from it. And if you get the chance to be with someone who is dying or who has recently died, I hope you can appreciate what a gift it can become to you. Touch us; weep with us; cherish the intertwining of our lives; and reflect on the mystery and joy of the one thing that all humans eventually have in common.

11 OPTIMISM

A lot of people are really gloomy about the state of the world. For example, my darling father occasionally opines that the world is going to hell in whatever a handbasket is. In vain may one point out that every generation since Plato has bewailed the fact that its leaders are knaves, its young fools, and modern life is rubbish. According to many people, the mead hall lies empty, the work of giants grows cold and decays, the raven stands guard on the ring-giver's grave (*nobody* put it better than the Anglo-Saxons!), and everything is going to shit.

This would be fine were it just restricted to septuagenarian males. However, Generations Y, Z and whatever comes next seem even worse afflicted. Younger people understandably point to uncertainty in the labour market, the cost of living and the civilisation-ending prophecies of the green movement. I was really saddened by the teenage daughter of a friend the other day telling me that she didn't want to have children because it would be so cruel to bring them up in a world facing war and climate Armageddon. And *all* of us in the West must sometimes despair of the shallowness we are bombarded with on our televisions and devices, which seems to orient us towards fame and money and short-term pleasures, simultaneously diminishing us and atomising us.

We humans are programmed to focus on the negative – to remember losses more than gains, and hardship more than comfort. That kept our ancestors alert and alive on the savannah. However, many developed countries today seem to be experiencing an epidemic of depression and pessimism and anger that simply isn't justified by the conditions we live in. And this is not only tragic for those caught up in it, but can also become – in the division and nihilism it can spawn – a negative feedback loop, a self-fulfilling prophecy.

It is certainly not my contention that the world is free from injustice, or that mankind doesn't need to live more sustainably, and a little righteous anger about such things may be necessary for action. But one thing that makes me happy as I approach death is the strong sense that things are not only ok but that they are improving.

DEATH AND EQUANIMITY

This is partly about perspective and gratitude, as I discussed above. Every time I go somewhere like Sierra Leone, I see people with the most horrendous histories of war, displacement and abuse, people with nothing to their names and few prospects of changing that, but with so much happiness and meaning and optimism in their lives that they radiate it to those around them. And at the same time I see people living in countries which others risk their lives to reach in a rickety dinghy just for the chance of a washing-up job, people benefiting from the greatest period of peace and prosperity in the history of our species, in a state of fury or dejection about the precise nature of one rich country's trading relationship with a club of other rich countries,* or which statues adorn the well-kept public spaces of their leafy town, or their bloody neighbour's refusal – *refusal* – to do something about his Japanese knotweed.

However, my optimism is also based on evidence. You might expect an aid worker like me to dwell on the misery, but (as Hans Rosling beautifully sets out in his book *Factfulness*) the world is getting better and will continue to do so, thanks to human ingenuity and cooperation. We are wealthier, healthier, happier, kinder, cleaner, more

---

* Bloody Brexit! But I bet you can't tell which way I voted.

peaceful, more equal and longer-lived than any previous generation. More kids reach their fifth birthdays, more women are educated, and the chance of dying in a war or a robbery or a storm is lower than ever before. The death rate from natural disasters has declined by 99 per cent since 1920. A car travelling at full speed today produces less pollution than a parked car in 1970. Almost 85 per cent of people now have access to electricity. Over 60 per cent of girls in low-income countries now finish primary school, and the average woman has been educated for nine years – just one short of the average man. The proportion of the world's population living in extreme poverty has halved in the past two decades. The average life expectancy of someone born today is well over 70. Malthus was wrong – we *can* feed 9 billion (and, contrary to the population-control lobby, isn't it also such a fantastic thing that so many more people will get a go on this incredible rollercoaster? We shouldn't hog it!).

Climate change is an enormous threat, and I don't want to underplay it. But I have a strong sense that the world – and nature – will survive it, and we will find ways to mitigate it. Our best minds are at last coming together to do something about it. My beloved Jersey is doing its bit in quite a big way in dairy, with cross-bred Jersey cows quadrupling milk yields in many parts of Africa. Already

DEATH AND EQUANIMITY

more and more land in Europe at least is being returned to nature from agriculture. And species are coming back from the brink as habitats are restored and we belatedly cooperate a bit better. Pandas and tigers and many types of whale are no longer listed as critically endangered on the IUCN Red List, and black rhino numbers are increasing in the wild. Through the cross-fertilisation of conservation and development programmes, poor people are being given an economic stake in the protection of the threatened ecosystems they inhabit.

It gives me a great sense of peace to think about how the world will continue after I'm gone. Children will want ice creams and people will fall head-over-heels in love and musicians will delight us and comedians will poke fun and people will tend their gardens and collect geeky things. If you can, ignore politics, consume much less news and try to stay away from social media. They all miss the big picture.

As I approach the end of my own self, I find the contemplation of other selves to be something enormously moving and comforting. I can get teary eyed watching kids walk to school clutching satchels, or people assembled with home-made signs to protest about something they care about, or reading a newspaper article about someone who's built a model of a church with matchsticks. (God, what an image you must by now have of me!) And, at the same time, I have resisted several calls from friends to try to record more about my own life, the escapades and fun and Withnailian feats of drinking. Tempting though that has sometimes been, it no longer seems relevant.

The point I'm trying to make was best expressed by Bertrand Russell, whom I will quote at length because it contains such a profound truth about the acceptance of death, about optimism, about connectedness and about other people. To overcome the fear of death, he suggests, we should widen our interests, and subsume them into the greater whole,

> until bit by bit the walls of the ego recede, and your life becomes increasingly merged in the universal life. An individual human existence should be like a river: small at first, narrowly contained within its banks, and rushing passionately past rocks and over waterfalls. Gradually the river grows wider, the banks recede, the waters flow more quietly, and in the end, without any visible break, they become merged in the sea, and painlessly lose their individual being. The man who, in old age, can see his life in this way, will not suffer from the fear of death, since the things he cares for will continue.

12 REGRETS AND BUCKET LISTS

I think there are really two types of regrets, and they can sometimes haunt both the dying and those with plenty of time left on the clock. The first are regrets about things we've done, and the second are those about things we didn't do.

I have several regrets about times I've behaved selfishly or stupidly. I left Oxford without finishing my degree and (much to the *delight* of my poor parents) went to work as a tour guide in Egypt. I dumped a girlfriend callously. I lost a dear friendship in a single night of ecstasy-fuelled lunacy in London. I scared off a wonderful German housemate in Ramallah by drunkenly holding a pistol to his head and telling him to stop leaving beard trimmings in the sink (done as a robust joke, I hasten to add, although those late-*intifada* days were wild). I prioritised my own need to have 'said goodbye' to a dying friend without thinking how sad and uncomfortable it made him. I nicked my mum's car and rolled it on the M3 motorway. Et cetera.

I know that everyone reading this can search their hearts and find the same. Seek forgiveness – unselfishly – if it helps, and apologise if you still can. Even better, make amends (though that's technically impossible – you can't 'amend' the past, but you can change the lens through which you and other people view it). All the 12-step programmes for addicts have this as part of the recovery and regeneration process, as do the amazing 'restorative justice' schemes which I mentioned above. But the main thing is to be able to live with yourself, and not to let these things eat at you. And a lot of that can be achieved simply through counselling, meditation or psychedelics. Moving on from regrets for things done is not selfish, and doesn't mean you blithely continue to behave like an arsehole. Being compassionate towards yourself is the *foundation* of being able to have compassion for others.

Regrets for things not done are more difficult, especially if you don't have time now to do them. According to end-of-life experts, this sadness about things which we failed to do is the lament that most commonly comes up on deathbeds. People wish they'd spent less time in the office and more with family, or been truer to themselves and quit

DEATH AND EQUANIMITY

that albatross job, or had the courage to move on from a destructive relationship.

The first remedy for this, of course, only applies to those who will go on living. Just think of yourself facing the end, and ask yourself what *you* will regret not having done. Benjamin Franklin observed that most people die at 25 but are not buried until they're 75. Now is the time, however old you are, to take stock and realise that life is precious and finite, and if you're prioritising status or wealth, or feeling stuck and loveless, or putting things off, or waiting until retirement (and the heart attack that will fell you before you *do* get to trek through Bhutan), you are not making the most of it. 'Aaaaalways remember,' (said Peter Cook, cruelly) 'if your life seems dull and dreary . . . it is.'

This doesn't mean you have to sell your house and buy that boat or motorhome (although a few people wrote to me after reading my newspaper scribblings to say they were doing something exactly like that). Travel. Find something new to do or to learn. Find a counsellor. Take magic mushrooms. Volunteer. Persevere with the dating (there *is* someone there for everyone). Work less hard, or at least from home sometimes. Spend the kids' inheritance (their true inheritance anyway is your love). As I said in my second article, but it's worth repeating, carpe that diem and keep it carped. And remember this maxim: if something's worth doing, it's worth doing *badly*. It's absolute rubbish that you need to excel at something for it to be worthwhile. Be crap at five-a-side, play the harmonica tunelessly, write shit poems for your family.

And whether you have time to do a lot or a little, thinking about that now-clichéd 'bucket list' can be a good place to start. I'm lucky not to have much on mine (I tell people I've always wanted to go seal-clubbing, which elicits mixed reactions). But there are loads of ideas on the internet, and the general principle is how can you best grab life by the genitals and squeeze joy out of it. The world is so full of opportunity and weirdness and colour, and it would be a shame to sleepwalk through this utterly improbable gift we've been given of simply existing at all. 'For there is good news yet to hear and fine things to be seen, before we go to Paradise by way of Kensal Green.'

A Beginner's Guide to Interacting with the Dying

I have received so much love and support over the relatively short period between diagnosis and dying, and it buoyed me enormously. As you may be bored of reading by now, I think human beings are fundamentally good, and the instinct to reach out and to provide comfort and assistance to people who are dying or suffering is a very fundamental one. I'm so grateful to all those who did so, for my wife and me; it made a tough journey significantly more bearable.

One problem I came to notice, though, is that while we want to help those in that situation, we don't always know how to do so. Stemming, I think, from our lack of practice at dealing with death, we sometimes say or do things which might actually be a bit crass or unhelpful. I have certainly done so myself in the past and, knowing what I know now, I cringe a little when I think about some of the worst examples.

A BEGINNER'S GUIDE TO DYING

This is a very short set of pointers, then, for those who are about to lose someone they care about. Or even just someone they know. It's very personal, and I don't presume to speak for everyone else in my boat. It also doesn't necessarily apply to dealing with the recently bereaved. I think there's probably some crossover, but there are many excellent and much more expertly written guides already out there for those circumstances. This just reflects what has helped me, and also explains the few occasions when I've had to draw upon reserves of humour to deal with something which unintentionally walloped me on the side of the head.

SOME DON'TS AND DOS

Again, dying people are not all the same, and the overarching piece of advice is to be guided by *them*. Some may want quotes from scripture or recommendations for new therapies or plenty of random people dropping by, and if so, please oblige! However, I've settled on these tips after discussion with a few fellow one-way visitors to Cancerland, and in the absence of other information I think they're a decent starting point. Remember that people in our situation may not have the strength to tell you otherwise, and may not want to risk offending you.

There are a few more Don'ts here than Dos, and some of them may even seem a bit uncharitable. If you've ever done any of them, please don't worry. I've done several myself, and I think the dying person always knows that behind them there is still something well-meant.

A BEGINNER'S GUIDE TO DYING

Do get in touch

This is the number one piece of advice: don't wait until it's too late, or worry about doing something wrong. It's wonderful to know that others are thinking of you, and indeed in a few cases I found myself thinking, 'Bloody hell, why haven't I heard from so-and-so?' I managed to get past that by reminding myself that people are scared of death, and of saying the wrong thing. Maybe my imminent death awakened some trauma, or they were going through a really difficult patch themselves (so, advice for the terminally ill: don't keep the score). However, it *is* nice to be contacted, and I loved receiving messages both from those I was still very close to and those with whom I hadn't spoken in 30 years.

When you make contact, though (and please message or write first, don't call on the phone out of the blue, for the same reasons as you shouldn't just turn up – see below), give a little thought to how it might come across. I present a few tips below, which also apply, of course, if you do meet in person.

INTERACTING WITH THE DYING

Don't just turn up unannounced

I was so lucky to have a very wide network of people I cared about a lot, but when one knows one is dying one needs to prioritise fairly ruthlessly, and to choreograph one's own remaining days as much as health and tedious medical procedures allow. An unexpected visit – or indeed a visit imposed with little warning – can be a colossal inconvenience both to the dying and their immediate family. Also, worse, it means one is probably going to have to have several hours either of great emotional intensity ('I've always wanted to tell you this . . .') or of awkward, subject-dodging bonhomie (it's really quite hard when facing the scythe to care hugely about someone else's children's exam results, or their recent trip to Morocco).

Visits in general are a tricky one. Some dying people will want lots (prearranged, of course) and some will want fewer, or none at all. My own problem has been that I *do* want to see everyone who suggests dropping by, but in general I don't want many visitors! You yourself are special to me, and I'd love a tea or a drink with you, but the same goes for perhaps 100 people, which then becomes unmanageable. I'm afraid I've been close to rude in putting people off. But please understand it's no reflection on you, or how much I value and love you.

And as for 'goodbyes', personally, apart from a very few of my immediate family, I found no need or desire for final farewells. Remember me from that weekend we spent together, or the time our fireworks burned down the neighbour's shed, not from a couple of hours when I'm feeling physically rotten. (Jersey Hospice is great at pretending there are visiting hours when actually there are none, just to ensure we have tranquillity when we need it!)

I would venture to say (and again, I've been guilty of it) that most final visits are ultimately more for the benefit of the visitor than the visited. So don't expect to come at all, let alone just hop in the car. Maybe offer once and immediately let it drop.

Don't skirt around the issue

All of us have different tolerances for directness or euphemism (personally I'd rather say 'died' than 'passed'), but you can gently broach the fact that you know the news isn't good, and even that time may well be short. This is not the time for a breezy email about something completely different (although a tiny bit of news is always welcome). Instead, if you write or message, consider bringing up some happy memories. Unlike in person or on the phone, where

INTERACTING WITH THE DYING

the recipient is on the spot, it might even be the moment to broach the topic that 'I've always wanted you to know...' (as long as it's not 'I slept with your wife in 2019').

Do listen!

This is a surprisingly difficult one for everyone, all the time. The fact is that in most conversations we are only half taking in what the person is saying, and the rest of the time thinking about what we will say back. A good half of training to be a Samaritan is devoted just to learning to listen to the person at the other end of the telephone. We all think we're good at it, and almost all of us are terrible!

People who are dying – or people who are dealing with a complex and scary new world of illness and treatment – are all different, but they are all trying to navigate something strange and frightening. I've lost count of the number of times I've tried to explain what's going on and how I feel about it, only to be floored by a comment which shows that none of it has sunk in. ('Oh yeah, Dad had pancreatic, but mercifully it only took three weeks.')

I'd like to quote here my friend Martin, a Falklands War hero in fact, who has advanced prostate cancer:

Listen – and listen carefully. It can be disconcerting to try to explain the complex and confusing world we now inhabit, and we might still be getting used to, only to be asked a question that tells me immediately you weren't listening.

Be patient and don't be frightened of silence. We may need time to think, or compose ourselves. Silence is fine between trusting friends – you don't have to keep thinking of things to say, because that will feel awkward. Cancer people want to talk when we're ready – we know you care and we are grateful for you giving us the time and chance to talk in our own way.

Give time and be kind. Most people are kind and thoughtful, underneath the cares of day-to-day life, so use that to be patient, and to remember, at least for now, this is about us, not you. Sorry to be selfish, but I cannot put it any other way.

Don't minimise things

However flippant I might be about my fate, be very careful about mirroring it. Just as certain words can now only be used by those they once were used against, dark humour is the preserve of the dying and not of the comforting. I might make jokes about '*Indignitas*' (the euthanasia clinic where they push you out of the window wearing a clown suit), or about wanting my ashes tossed into the eyes of a peloton of cyclists, but you probably shouldn't, even if you know me really well.

Also, avoid any sentence which starts with 'at least'. I've had some corkers, and am lucky they amuse me, but dying people don't want to hear that at least they'll avoid the indignities of old age, at least they'll be in a better place, at least they've paid off their mortgage, or at least they won't have to vote in the next election.

A variant on both skirting and minimising, which my wife and I had a *lot*, was people insisting that against all the odds I'd recover. It reminds me of a probably embellished story about King George V, who almost on his deathbed was reportedly told he'd soon be well again and be able to take in the delights of the seaside town Bognor Regis. His response was simply, 'Bugger Bognor.'

People usually mean well when they say that somehow the palliative radiotherapy you're having for the pain might cure you, or that their cousin's dog-groomer went into remission overnight against all medical expectations, but it comes across as you not listening to me. Your refusal to accept my predicament isn't kind; it smacks of you ducking the issue (and maybe more for your benefit than mine). If the dying person is still a Panglossian optimist then do go along with it, but otherwise bugger that.

Don't put too much onus on people to reply

It's lovely to get a message saying 'no need to respond to this' because quite often one doesn't have either the energy or the mental bandwidth to do so. For that reason, it's often best not to ask any questions, because people feel they need to supply an answer. As well as emails and letters, this particularly goes for platforms like Facebook and WhatsApp. 'Thinking of you today' is much better than 'How did chemo go?' Anything which can be replied to with a simple 'thanks' or heart emoji conveys all that love and support without creating an obligation.

Don't offer medical advice

Don't make specific enquiries about our health, and for goodness' sake avoid touting any treatments. It's not nice to be asked details about bone metastases, or the particulars of any therapy we're undergoing (usually painful and often undignified). Worst, though, is being sent advice or miracle cures.

I can only speak for cancer, but a very edited list of the treatments or medicines I've been advised includes black-seed oil, apricots, cherries, turmeric, honey, bicarbonate of soda, a sugar-free diet, numerous off-label drugs and a concoction of herbs only found in Namibia. While there may well be little-known things which will one day be shown to be of benefit, there probably isn't a global conspiracy by 'Big Pharma' to keep you from accessing them (after all, there's still a Nobel Prize in it for the first person to prove any of these things are effective). Personally, my default position is that brilliant Tim Minchin quote: 'You know what they call alternative medicine which has been proved to work? Medicine!'

There's also a tendency (and again, I've done it myself) to remind people of the importance of staying positive. There's actually no scientific evidence that doing so makes any difference at all to a patient's outcomes (though it's *so* helpful to one's quality of life), but most importantly it's often rather difficult when you are full of tubes and contemplating how your parents will cope with you dying before them. At best it can be a bit hollow, but at worst it can make the dying feel guilty that they're doing something wrong. And telling someone to 'stay positive' of course has no actual power to make them do so.

New scientific treatments are perhaps harder. I do understand the need to share something you believed worked for someone you know's sister, and there are certainly trials going on now in most diseases for drugs which will be mainstream in a few years' time. I also know plenty of cancer patients who are desperate to try anything at all, and zoom around from the new proton beam therapy in Hamburg to the pioneering immunologist in Estonia. However, my own advice would be to be very careful recommending these (particularly if you're not a doctor yourself, but just read about them in the newspaper).

After a shaky start, medically, I was so happy to have a team of doctors which I trusted. For me one of the biggest benefits was to be able to let them worry about my care – being confident that they would find any clinical trials or medicines that might genuinely buy a few months – and to pass that whole mental burden onto them. When a dying patient is bombarded with well-intended recommendations, it puts it all back on them again ('Damn – maybe I *should* have tried that new chemo protocol in Istanbul which Susan sent me'). It also means that you haven't really acknowledged that we are, indeed, dying.

INTERACTING WITH THE DYING

Don't force religion (or lack of it) onto anyone

Again, I see the temptation – your belief system has helped *you* so much, and you want the person you love to feel those benefits as well. Also, as they approach the end of their lives, many people – myself included – become more interested in matters of the spirit and the soul. This isn't a clutching at straws, or a last punt on Pascal's Wager, but it comes quite naturally when one can finally see death clearly, unhidden at last from all our terrors and taboos. But please be careful, and take your lead from the person who is dying.

Personally, in my last few months I enjoyed engaging in religious discussions with a few people whose opinions I really valued. I also enjoyed looking at different belief systems. But you're unlikely to help anyone much with quotes from the Bible or the Koran, or YouTube videos of preachers, and you're very unlikely indeed to help anyone in any way if you recommend any form of miraculous healing. You run the risk of causing offence, by inadvertently suggesting that someone has been wrong all these years. And by awakening or feeding a sense of false hope in someone, you are potentially creating an obstacle to what I found was the most beneficial thing of all when facing death: coming simply to accept it.

Equally, if you're a committed ostrich-headed Dawkins atheist (as I was for several years), now's not the moment to tell someone (as I was told) that they're no more important than 'a squashed insect'.

I am actually grateful for two emails in particular, because they made me laugh a lot. One said very matter-of-factly that I may have lived a good life, but I was certainly going to hell, and the other just started 'Get down on your knees!' But not everyone will love that. If you do fervently believe in something, by all means offer to talk about it. But then step back.

Do offer help – but be specific

People around us in Jersey – and even further afield – were so kind in the support they provided my wife and me. The lawn got mowed, the dog got walked, and food would just appear on the doorstep. Someone even rented scaffolding and fixed our roof after a big storm. If you offer help, try to think of something in particular which will be useful. I realise that over the years I must have sent dozens of messages which included the line 'please let me know if there's anything I can do', and unsurprisingly nobody ever took me up on it. The reason is that when you're dying it's often quite hard to ask anyway, and also you hesitate to go back to those general offers with specific requests because you don't really know how sincere they were.

What can you really do to help, beyond (most importantly of all) just gently letting someone know they are in your thoughts? Maybe it's the school run or a frozen lasagne. Maybe it's proposing to let other people in a particular friendship group know how they're doing, so the dying person doesn't have to tell everyone separately. Maybe it's offering – but not insisting on – a chat or a cup of tea on a specified afternoon (I also used to wonder why 'Do call any time' got no responses). But if you genuinely mean it, think of something relatively specific that might help, and make it as easy as possible for the dying person to say either yes or no.

And finally, on this topic, a tip for the dying. People really do want to help, and (if you can) it's good to overcome the knee-jerk reaction (it was mine for a while, anyway) to turn everything down. For one thing, it's actually rather kind to other people to give them ways they can feel useful, and for another there are certainly things you could use a hand with. As with those offering, my advice is to be specific. Suggesting small, low-cost things which are genuinely helpful and not onerous to you are wonderful ways to bring you closer to the many people who love you (and there are many: many more than you probably even know), and who feel helpless in the face of this awful thing you're going through. Just resist the temptation to tell them you need a new TV, or that your dog's anal glands need expressing.

Recommended Reading

Below are a few books which have influenced my thinking on some of the subjects above, and which I recommend.

The Rational Optimist: How Prosperity Evolves by Matt Ridley

The Better Angels of Our Nature: Why Violence Has Declined by Steven Pinker

Enlightenment Now: The Case for Reason, Science, Humanism and Progress by Steven Pinker

Factfulness: Ten Reasons We're Wrong About the World – and Why Things Are Better Than You Think by Hans Rosling

Humankind: A Hopeful History by Rutger Bregman

Being Mortal: Illness, Medicine and What Matters in the End by Atul Gwande

How to Change Your Mind: What the New Science of Psychedelics Teaches Us About Consciousness, Dying, Addiction, Depression, and Transcendence by Michael Pollan

A BEGINNER'S GUIDE TO DYING

The Lives of a Cell: Notes of a Biology Watcher by Lewis Thomas

A Brief History of Everyone Who Ever Lived: The Stories in Our Genes by Adam Rutherford

Anam Cara: A Book of Celtic Wisdom by John O'Donohue

Why Buddhism is True: The Science and Philosophy of Meditation and Enlightenment by Robert Wright

Man's Search for Meaning by Viktor Frankl

Waking Up: A Guide to Spirituality Without Religion by Sam Harris

Radical Acceptance: Embracing Your Life With the Heart of a Buddha by Tara Brach

With the End in Mind: Dying, Death and Wisdom in an Age of Denial by Kathryn Mannix

Unapologetic: Why, Despite Everything, Christianity Can Still Make Surprising Emotional Sense by Francis Spufford

The Book: On the Taboo Against Knowing Who You Are by Alan Watts

A Short Chronology

1977
Born in London, to Sarah and Tony Boas
Sister Julia follows in 1980

1982–4
Dulwich Village Infants School

1984–90
Dulwich College Preparatory School
Head Boy and Chief Librarian!

1990–95
Winchester College

1995–6
Gap Year in Vietnam
Taught at Saigon Children's Charity and sub-edited the Saigon Times

1996–2000
Brasenose College, Oxford University, reading English Literature
Left without completing degree

2001–3
Tour Guide in Egypt, Turkey and India
Two years in Egypt

2004
Bir Zeit University, Palestine
Studied Arabic

2004–8
Palestine Economic Policy Research Institute
Programme Coordinator and Researcher

2006–7
Bath University, studying International Policy Analysis
MSc

2008
Palestinian Ministry of Planning
Special adviser to the Minister. Helped write Gaza reconstruction plan

2009
PlaNet Finance
Country Director

2010
Married Aurélie
The soulmate I'd fallen in love with on a bus in 2008

2010–12
UN Food and Agriculture Organisation (FAO): Head of Gaza Office
Lived in Gaza for 2.5 years, commuting at the weekends to the West Bank

2012–14
UN FAO Nepal: managing large project on transboundary animal diseases
Based in Kathmandu but responsible for eight South Asian countries

2014–16
UK Civil Service
Various roles in business, health and customs

2016–24
Director of Jersey Overseas Aid
Selected and managed about £100m of grants to development charities

2019–
Samaritan

2020–
Jersey Heritage, Trustee and then Chair (2023–)

2021–
Constable's Officer
Volunteer policeman, alongside Aurélie

Random Facts

Height
Six foot six inches in the mornings

Countries lived in
UK, Vietnam, Egypt, Turkey, India, Palestine, Nepal, Jersey

Other countries worked in
Cambodia, Oman, Jordan, Lebanon, Thailand, Bhutan, Sri Lanka, Rwanda, Malawi, Sierra Leone, Zambia, Ethiopia, Ukraine, Switzerland, Poland

Cigarettes
c.200,000

Nickname
Bob

Bears outside tent
Twice

Tigers in the wild
Nine occasions

Arrests made
Zero. Once turned on blue lights and siren

Detained by police
UK, Croatia, Israel, Vietnam

Favourite poem
'Fern Hill', by Dylan Thomas

Favourite Food
Cheese fondue

A BEGINNER'S GUIDE TO DYING

Rude Poem
'Cyclists are C**ts', now illustrated and available on Amazon. Please only search it out if you're not easily offended and can tolerate awful language

Sailing
c.10,000 miles

Shot
Once. Israeli army, Qalandia Checkpoint, 2004. Back of the leg. Good war wound until someone pointed out I must have been running away

Guns owned
12-bore shotgun, .22 LR target pistol, CZ 9 mm, .357 Magnum revolver

Random UK jobs
Care home cleaner, prison clerk, special needs teaching assistant, barman, jacuzzi installer, removals man, 'lambing lad', tractor driver

Nationalities at wedding
24

Favourite Choirs sung in
Zaridash (West Bank), Kathmandu Chorale (Nepal)

Strip searches at Ben Gurion airport
c.30, with a short break while enjoying diplomatic immunity for three years

Awards
Bailiff's Silver Seal, Jersey. World Jersey Cattle Bureau 'Certificate of Achievement' for services to the Jersey breed in Africa

Letters in *The Times*
Eleven, including the coveted bottom right-hand corner

Dog
Pippin, a Picardy Shepherd. 2019–

Hymns at funeral
'Dear Lord and Father of Mankind', 'Guide Me Oh Thou Great Redeemer', 'Lead, Kindly Light'

Epilogue: Excerpts from Simon's Eulogy
BY HIS OLDEST FRIEND JAMES
Trinity Church, Jersey, August 2024

I would like to start by thanking Simon for asking me to say a few words about him, not least because it means he didn't follow up on an earlier instruction that at his funeral I absolutely had to sing 'Walking in the Air' in the style of a 14-year old Aled Jones.

Like many of you, I have been amazed in the past few months that, in the face of recent experiences, Simon retained the equilibrium and clarity of mind to write so many words that inspired so many. If you haven't read his articles in the *Jersey Evening Post* you are not one of the hundreds of thousands who have, or who have heard him speak about his situation on the radio, on Broadcasting House and the *Today* programme. He was also just a little smug to have reached double figures for letters published in *The Times*. I haven't counted the number of times Simon mentioned Muscadet in all these pieces but it certainly guaranteed a steady supply of bottles sent by grateful readers in the last couple of months.

For myself, I have been prone to dwell on the things that won't now happen, the places he won't see, the people he won't meet, but it was Simon himself who said to me James, *habibi*, think of all the things we have done, the life we have led. And what a life it was.

Simon's hard-wired desire for freedom and love of travel started early.

Looking back, his parents were unusually trusting, incredibly so by modern standards, and he was allowed at age 13 to go cycling round France with a friend, followed by similar trips to Holland, then interrailing around Europe at 14 and 15.

In 1993, at 16, Simon did his first overseas aid work, taking a convoy of donated goods with a group from the Catholic Church to a refugee camp near Mostar in Bosnia. This experience, seeing war close up, meeting the ethnically cleansed, was to be a formative influence on him.

In 1996, in his gap year, Simon flew to Saigon, where he volunteered as an English teacher with the Saigon Children's Charity, working in a slum in District 4. In the

EPILOGUE: EXCERPTS FROM SIMON'S EULOGY

evenings he sub-edited the *Saigon Times* and played pool at Long Phi bar surrounded by a merry band of misfits. I joined him later in the year, more at the bar than at the charity despite it appearing on my CV for years to come, and we drove old Russian Minsk motorbikes around the country, periodically falling off and arriving in villages in the Mekong Delta at 20mph on our bottoms. Crossing the border to Cambodia during the coup d'état of 1997, a period so dangerous that no right-minded person would go there, we found we had the Angkor Wat Temple complex to ourselves. To the bemusement of our drivers, Simon insisted we visit each site in chronological order, making stoned geeky notes on Khmer architecture, and using catapults to shoot frogs in the deserted temple ponds.

A story Simon loved to recount from this time involved him being separated from me and our friend Chinh while biking along the border. Not sure which country he was actually in, and with the Khmer Rouge still active, he was caught in a massive thunderstorm and decided he'd have to get off the road. Clad in a pink plastic poncho, he drove into a hut, stopped his engine and tried to explain to the bewildered villagers – who may not have seen a Westerner since 1975, let alone one measuring six foot six – that he needed shelter from the lightning and monsoon rain. To break the ice, he produced a magic trick, which involved taking a curtain ring off a length of string tied around a very nervous woman's wrists. However, as his eyes accustomed to the gloom, he became aware that there was a dead body on a bed, and it slowly dawned that he had driven into a wake. He started his engine and drove out into the tempest, leaving the villagers wondering who that strange, pink ghost might have been.

Simon read English Literature at Oxford from 1996–2000, repeating his last year after a minor car accident, but in the end not finishing his degree. He later confided that this was one of the best things he ever did. It burnt all the conventional bridges and enabled him to focus on seeing the world as he wanted, and living off his wits. He took up tour guiding in Egypt for a couple of years, followed by India, then Turkey.

In 2004 he studied Arabic at Bir Zeit University in the West Bank and pursued more charitable work as a programme coordinator and researcher at the Palestine Economic Policy Research Institute. He was very proud to have attended Yassir Arafat's funeral, a personal gesture which secretly amused him when he was in groups brandishing more ostentatious pro-Palestinian credentials.

Simon returned to England in 2006, attending Bath University to study International Policy Analysis, and earned a Master's with Distinction. When he told me

EPILOGUE: EXCERPTS FROM SIMON'S EULOGY

this news he added two exclamation marks for emphasis. There he made rich and long-lasting friendships. In fact, as all here know well, it is notable that everywhere Simon has travelled and studied, he has accumulated a long tail of friends, loyal and loving.

Following this brief sojourn home, Simon returned again to the Middle East, becoming special adviser to the Palestinian Ministry of Planning, and it was here, in 2008, on the airport bus, that he met his soulmate, Aurélie, newly arrived from France to study journalism. They fell in love and they have been together, adoring and adored, ever since. In 2013, after three years in the Food and Agricultural Office for the UN in Gaza, Aurélie and Simon moved to Kathmandu, where he ran a UN project on transboundary animal diseases covering the whole of South Asia, and where they would enjoy exploring and trekking together in the mountains. Seeking a more structured professional environment, Simon followed this with a brief stint in the Civil Service in the UK, which gave them time to pause and think where to take their lives next, reflecting that it was perhaps time to stop living with six security guards in their house.

It was the Civil Service training that introduced Simon and Aurélie to Jersey, where they settled in 2016 and made their home. Simon loved living in this close-knit community surrounded by wonderful and interesting people, and has described the wonderful feeling of acceptance and welcome he and Aurélie have always felt here. He ran Jersey Overseas Aid in partnership with the Minister for International Development, doubling its budget and focusing aid on what Jersey is really good at: dairy, finance and conservation. Only Simon could find himself in a role that involved exporting cow semen, but it turned out this was a serious endeavour and he frequently travelled out to Rwanda, among other African countries, and was immensely proud of the herds he helped seed, forging close links with the farmers he met.

Simon embraced many aspects of life on Jersey. Together with Aurélie, he became an honorary police officer – many here might not have placed him in the *front* seat of a police car; he has been a Samaritan since 2019 and chaired Jersey Heritage Trust. In May he was awarded the Bailiff's Silver Seal for his inspirational contribution to the island, through voluntary work and latterly his sharing of his journey with the world via the *Jersey Evening Post*. He claimed also to be the undisputed Scrabble champion of the island although, I should add, this is not something I have been able to independently verify.

Which brings me to Simon's character, the man behind all this. I remember deciding with him in our early

EPILOGUE: EXCERPTS FROM SIMON'S EULOGY

twenties that if we lost everything, were down on our luck and in the gutter, we would still have our sense of humour. Nobody could take that from us, nor change the absurd lens through which we observed the world. And with all the tributes and testimonies that have come in in recent weeks, what shines through is how much fun we all enjoyed with him, the countless ridiculous situations and scrapes we ended up in, the laughter we shared with him.

For Simon, the world was out there to be explored, examined, mostly parodied and never taken too seriously. And one thing I will always treasure was the mischievous glint in his eyes when he realised people could not be sure if he was being extremely rude, gently mocking, or simply joking.

Simon had a particular knack for disarming people, either by charm or by confusion or a combination of both. When driving up to checkpoints, always potential flashpoints in the Middle East, he would ingenuously ask stern-faced guards for directions, or for interesting information, such as the precise number of kilometres to the next town, which is still one of the few Arabic phrases I can remember. Immediately any tension would drain away, as the guards found themselves useful and authoritative and ushered us on with goodwill.

Not that this approach always worked. On a visit to Lebanon around this time, we decided to tour the country by car, despite it taking us several days to leave the bar in Beirut early enough in the day to hire one. After we had visited the Beqaa valley and the temple of Jupiter at Baalbek, Simon thought nothing of driving us towards the southern border with Israel, an area controlled by Hezbollah and on a road generally considered impassable. You couldn't help noticing that the number of roadside posters of martyrs increased with every village we passed. Being in our twenties and beyond the age of reason we were, naturally, in an open-topped Mercedes blaring Western pop songs, but Simon approached the checkpoint with a broad smile and an air of 'just passing through, thanks', until it was politely but firmly suggested by the heavily armed guards that we turn around and cross the Litani river further up to reach the coast. Well, you can't win them all.

I'd like to leave you with Simon's own words about death, sent accidentally, unintentionally, although, as it turned out, prophetically, in 2021:

> Try not to grieve. For a few years yet I will exist in memory, but don't let these thoughts be sad ones. Think of your own life like a book. For some people I am a chapter; for others I am a paragraph or a footnote. But please think of the Simon section of your history with happiness, and move on. Your

EPILOGUE: EXCERPTS FROM SIMON'S EULOGY

book is your own. And for goodness' sake don't let the thinking about an essentially happy chapter mar the rest of it – that really doesn't make sense. My life was pretty great – so smile about it!

Our dear Simon, you have given us all so much joy and happiness, and memories to last forever. Rest in peace, dear friend. You left this world happy and content, and we are assured that when our time is up, you will be waiting for us, Scrabble board and glass of Muscadet in hand, to entertain us again.

Final Word

I am almost certainly going to die in the next fortnight, thanks in the end to my blood calcium levels, which no longer respond to any drug. Not a bad way to go, though I'm not much looking forward to the period of dementia that apparently comes with it!

I've been tremendously lucky to have had this final period of pause and reflection. I've enjoyed the fact that I could work (at home at least) for Jersey Overseas Aid and Jersey Heritage. I even did a police patrol with the squad car and in full uniform, though I stopped on a single-track lane to pick some flowers and realised, when I had unwittingly created a traffic jam, that this was probably a rather odd sight!

Most of all, though, I was able to spend some special time with Aurélie, talking about important things, laughing and crying, and wondering why Muscadet bottles seem to have shrunk in size.

I've dealt with a few regrets, I've corresponded with people from all over the world who had read my newspaper articles, and we managed even to escape to France a couple of times (again, thanks to Jersey Hospice and my wonderful oncologist, who rearranged things and pumped me full of a few helpful drugs). I've chosen some hymns and poems for my funeral, and a simple limestone headstone (I *want* it to discolour and fade).

The sense of peace I've been blessed with, even of joy, has not been dimmed at all. Despite some additional pain from the bones, and the recent propensity of the tumour poking out through my feeding stoma to turn the kitchen into a scene from *Reservoir Dogs*, I've been as happy as I've ever been in my life. I have so many things and people to thank for this, but I hope that some of what I've set out above will also make the same thing possible for you when your turn comes.

Thanks and Acknowledgements

It is really difficult to write a 'thanks' section because I'm grateful to so many people, and it's very hard not to make this as long as the book itself. I don't mention individual friends or neighbours or colleagues, who have been the most wonderful sources of support and good humour. In one sense, even, everyone I've ever met or worked with has contributed to where I am today (literally sitting in the sun with an idiotic smile on my face). However, I think it's right to highlight a few people who have helped with this book and my care over the past few weeks.

Gill Coleridge has been absolutely instrumental in helping me turn scribblings into something publishable. Not only have her deep knowledge and long career in the book world helped me deal with publishers, but I've so appreciated the long daily chats with my wonderful godmother.

Mark Richards and the team at Swift have been astonishing from the moment they read the manuscript. Their palpable enthusiasm for what I have written was as important to me as the fact they were able to move so quickly. It's been so good to be able to make a few last decisions, and even to see the cover! It's nice to die knowing my words are in such good hands.

I should also mention Susanna Wadeson at Penguin/Doubleday, who was the first person to approach me (after my second newspaper piece) and suggest I might work that up into something longer, and who has been so helpful and encouraging throughout. The *Daily Telegraph* has also been incredibly enthusiastic, in particular Louise Carpenter, who interviewed me for the paperback in May and who has become a great friend since.

I'd like to thank the *Jersey Evening Post*, and in particular its genius editor Andy Sibcy, who has encouraged me from when I first asked if I could write about my illness, and who has been so generous with rights and photographs. Local newspapers are the lifeblood of a community, and Jersey is so fortunate to have such a good one.

A few readers have helped me include some important topics (and commas), and to make me sound less bonkers. In particular, these were my sister Julia, my cousin Imogen, and my friends Aurélie Vandeputte, Andy Parker and Tom Powell.

THANKS AND ACKNOWLEDGEMENTS

My colleagues at Jersey Overseas Aid are more like a family than workmates. They have made the last couple of months so easy as I transitioned from hands-on director to floaty, online decision-maker, while also grieving my imminent death. Likewise, I am so grateful to the JOA 'Commissioners' (my board) and my very amazing boss, Jersey's Minister for International Development, Carolyn Labey. I am so proud of what we all built there together, and it gives me such pleasure to know what good hands that brilliant organisation is in.

I want to thank my oncologist, Dr Elizabet Gomes dos Santos, and my palliative care consultant, Dr Nicky Bailhache. They have both dealt with *me* and not just my disease, while also treating the cancer and its symptoms so expertly. They have enabled me not to think about the medical side, which lifted a huge mental load from my shoulders. And the lovely, joyful, professional nurses at both the oncology centre at the hospital and at Jersey Hospice have meant that every visit is a joy. So much laughter!

Finally, I want readers to be aware of how grateful I am to Aurélie, to Mum and Dad, and to Julia. This isn't a direct thank-you to them as they already know how grateful I am, but their love and support and good humour when they are faced with such an awful loss have been inspirational.

ALSO AVAILABLE FROM
Vintage Books

HOW WE DIE
Reflections on Life's Final Chapter
by Sherwin B. Nuland

Even more relevant than when it was first published, this edition addresses contemporary issues in end-of-life care and includes an all-embracing and incisive afterword that examines the state of health care and our relationship with life as it approaches its terminus. A National Book Award winner, *How We Die* also discusses how we can take control of our own final days and those of our loved ones.

Medicine

THE DIVING BELL AND THE BUTTERFLY
A Memoir of Life in Death
by Jean-Dominique Bauby

In 1995, Jean-Dominique Bauby was the editor in chief of French *Elle* and the father of two young children—a forty-four-year-old man known and loved for his wit, his style, and his impassioned approach to life. By the end of the year he was also the victim of a rare kind of stroke. After twenty days in a coma, Bauby awoke into a body that had all but stopped working: only his left eye functioned, allowing him to see and, by blinking it, to make clear that his mind was unimpaired. Almost miraculously, he was soon able to express himself in the richest detail. By turns wistful, mischievous, angry, and witty, Bauby bears witness to his determination to live as fully in his mind as he had been able to do in his body. Again and again he returns to an "inexhaustible reservoir of sensations," keeping in touch with himself and the life around him. Bauby died two days after the French publication of this title. This book is a lasting testament to his life.

Memoir

THE YEAR OF MAGICAL THINKING
by Joan Didion

Several days before Christmas 2003, John Gregory Dunne and Joan Didion saw their only daughter fall ill. She was put into an induced coma and placed on life support. Days later, the Dunnes were sitting down to dinner after visiting the hospital when John suffered a massive and fatal coronary. In a second, this close, symbiotic partnership of forty years was over. Four weeks later, their daughter pulled through. Two months after that, she collapsed and underwent six hours of brain surgery at UCLA Medical Center to relieve a massive hematoma. This powerful book is Didion's attempt to make sense of the "weeks and then months that cut loose any fixed idea I ever had about death, about illness . . . about marriage and children and memory . . . about the shallowness of sanity, about life itself."

Memoir

NOTHING TO BE FRIGHTENED OF
by Julian Barnes

A memoir on mortality as only Julian Barnes can write it, one that touches on faith, science, and family, as well as a rich array of exemplary figures who have confronted the same questions he now poses about the most basic fact of life: its inevitable extinction. If the fear of death is "the most rational thing in the world," how does one contend with it? Deadly serious, masterfully playful, and surprisingly hilarious, *Nothing to Be Frightened Of* is a riveting display of how this supremely gifted writer goes about his business and a highly personal tour of the human condition and what might follow the final diagnosis.

Biography/Memoir

VINTAGE BOOKS
Available wherever books are sold.
vintagebooks.com

9/25

Culpeper County Library
271 Southgate Shopping Center
Culpeper, Virginia 22701
(540) 825-8691

WITHDRAWN